AISyS 2024

The First International Conference on AI-based Systems and Services

September 29 - October 03, 2024

Venice, Italy

AISyS 2024 Editors

Erik Buchmann, Leipzig University, Germany

Dennis Hoppe, HLRS, University of Stuttgart, Germany

Printed from e-media with permission by:

Curran Associates, Inc.
57 Morehouse Lane
Red Hook, NY 12571

Some format issues inherent in the e-media version may also appear in this print version.

International Academy, Research, and Industry Association (IARIA)
412 Derby Way
Wilmington, DE 19810

Phone: (408) 893-6407
Fax: (408) 527-6351

petre@iaria.org

Additional copies of this publication are available from:

Curran Associates, Inc.
57 Morehouse Lane
Red Hook, NY 12571 USA
Phone: 845-758-0400
Fax: 845-758-2633
Email: curran@proceedings.com
Web: www.proceedings.com

Table of Contents

AISyS 2024

Forward

The First International Conference on AI-based Systems and Services (AISyS 2024), held on September 29 – October 3, 2024 in Venice, Italy, initiated a series of events covering a broad spectrum of AI centered topics.

AI-based solutions for monitoring, control, decision making are expected to increase the capability of systems providing mechanism for predictions, optimization, risk minimization by interpreting situations and large volumes of data.

A variety of domains (Ambiental, Tactile, Language Processing, Tracking, Healthcare, Ecology, etc.) expanded in the last years based on practical advances provided by Artificial Intelligence (AI). Machine learning AI-based discovery and learning allow deep-learning (and unlearn obsolete knowledge), accurate forecasts, fault prevention and detection, as well as prediction of special diseases. Practical AI-based services in Internet of Things (IoT), Transportation systems, Cyber-systems, Citizen-centric systems, and others reached new levels of usability and quality.

The conference had the following tracks:

- Core AI-features
- AI-based systems
- AI-based societal services

This event was very competitive in its selection process and very well perceived by the international AI community. As such, it is attracting excellent contributions and active participation from all over the world. We were very pleased to receive a large amount of top quality contributions.

We take here the opportunity to warmly thank all the members of the AISyS 2024 technical program committee as well as the numerous reviewers. The creation of such a broad and high quality conference program would not have been possible without their involvement. We also kindly thank all the authors that dedicated much of their time and efforts to contribute to the AISyS 2024. We truly believe that thanks to all these efforts, the final conference program consists of top quality contributions.

This event could also not have been a reality without the support of many individuals, organizations and sponsors. We also gratefully thank the members of the AISyS 2024 organizing committee for their help in handling the logistics and for their work that is making this professional meeting a success.

We hope the AISyS 2024 was a successful international forum for the exchange of ideas and results between academia and industry and to promote further progress in AI-based systems and services research. We also hope that Venice provided a pleasant environment during the conference and everyone saved some time for exploring this beautiful city

AISyS 2024 General Chair

Steve Chan, Decision Engineering Analysis Laboratory, USA

AISyS 2024 Steering Committee

Michael Resch, University of Stuttgart, High Performance Computing Center, Germany
H.B. Acharya, Rochester Institute of Technology, USA
Erik Buchmann, Center for Scalable Data Analytics and Artificial Intelligence, Germany
Marc Kurz, University of Applied Sciences Upper Austria, Austria
Ahsan Pervaiz, Google Cloud, USA

AISyS 2024 Publicity Chair

Lorena Parra Boronat, Universitat Politecnica de Valencia, Spain
Sandra Viciano Tudela, Universitat Politecnica de Valencia, Spain
Jose Miguel Jimenez, Universitat Politecnica de Valencia, Spain
Francisco Javier Díaz Blasco, Universitat Politecnica de Valencia, Spain
Ali Ahmad, Universitat Politecnica de Valencia, Spain

AISyS 2024

Committee

AISyS 2024 General Chair

Steve Chan, Decision Engineering Analysis Laboratory, USA

AISyS 2024 Steering Committee

Michael Resch, University of Stuttgart, High Performance Computing Center, Germany
H.B. Acharya, Rochester Institute of Technology, USA
Erik Buchmann, Center for Scalable Data Analytics and Artificial Intelligence, Germany
Marc Kurz, University of Applied Sciences Upper Austria, Austria
Ahsan Pervaiz, Google Cloud, USA

AISyS 2024 Publicity Chair

Lorena Parra Boronat, Universitat Politecnica de Valencia, Spain
Sandra Viciano Tudela, Universitat Politecnica de Valencia, Spain
Jose Miguel Jimenez, Universitat Politecnica de Valencia, Spain
Francisco Javier Díaz Blasco, Universitat Politecnica de Valencia, Spain
Ali Ahmad, Universitat Politecnica de Valencia, Spain

AISyS 2024 Technical Program Committee

Manoj Acharya, SRI International, USA
Varol Akman, Ihsan Dogramaci Bilkent University, Turkey
Michael Atighetchi, Raytheon BBN Technologies, USA
Erik Buchmann, Center for Scalable Data Analytics and Artificial Intelligence, Germany
Steve Chan, Decision Engineering Analysis Laboratory, USA
Shuaichen Chang, The Ohio State University / Amazon Web Services, USA
Jinglin Chen, TikTok Inc., USA
Sam Cheng, University of Illinois Urbana-Champaign, USA
Mohammed Dahane, Université de Lorraine, France
Charalampos Dimoulas, Aristotle University, Greece
Mounim A. El Yacoubi, Institut Polytechnique de Paris, France
Alain-Jerome Fougeres, ECAM Rennes, France
Yannick Fourastier, Codeurope, Ukraine
Ivan Ganchev, University of Limerick, Ireland / Plovdiv University, Bulgaria
Ilche Georgievski, University of Stuttgart, Germany
Ashish Gupta, BITS Pilani Dubai Campus, UAE
Tzung-Pei Hong, National University of Kaohsiung, Taiwan
Zhipeng Huang, Case Western Reserve University, USA
Ehsan Kazemi, University of Central Florida, USA

Copyright Information

An Advanced Surrogate Model Approach for Enhancing Fluid Dynamics Simulations

Shubham Kavane, Kajol Kulkarni, Harald Köstler
Chair of System Simulation, Friedrich Alexander Universität Erlangen-Nürnberg
Erlangen, Germany
e-mail: {shubham.kavane, kajol.kulkarni, harald.koestler}@fau.de

***Abstract*—The increasing complexity and computational demands of 3D fluid dynamics simulations highlight the need for advanced surrogate models that strike a balance between predictive accuracy, computational efficiency, and convergence time. Traditional Computational Fluid Dynamics (CFD) methods, while highly accurate, are often resource-intensive and time-consuming. This research presents advanced U-Net-based surrogate models for 3D fluid flow prediction, aiming to achieve faster convergence and more efficient resource utilization while retaining competitive accuracy relative to traditional CFD solvers. We developed a U-Net model featuring an improved architecture utilizing an advanced attention mechanism known as the Convolution Block Attention mechanism. Considering the high computational demands, the model was trained using multiple GPUs, incorporating both model and data parallelism techniques. The model's capability was evaluated through overfitting experiments, where it was trained on a limited dataset to assess its ability to accurately replicate true labels. These findings highlight the promise of advanced surrogate models as a viable alternative to traditional CFD methods, providing faster solutions and reduced computational costs with comparable accuracy. Future research will focus on evaluating the current advanced U-Net model, trained on an extensive dataset of 10,000 samples, against Fourier Neural Operators and traditional CFD solvers in terms of training time, accuracy, and resource utilization, including energy consumption.**

Keywords-Surrogate Models; Computational Fluid Dynamics (CFD); U-Net; Fourier Neural Operators; Model Parallelism;

I. INTRODUCTION

The rapid advancements in Machine Learning (ML) and Deep Learning (DL) have transformed various fields by providing innovative solutions to complex problems once considered unsolvable. These technologies have revolutionized applications across various scientific domains [1]. Notably, in fluid dynamics, ML and DL have introduced groundbreaking methods that enhance our ability to understand and tackle intricate challenges, underscoring their profound and far-reaching impact [2].

Traditional fluid flow analysis relies on the Navier-Stokes equations (NSE), which, despite their strong theoretical foundation, are time-consuming and computationally intensive, particularly for complex scenarios. The limited parallelizability and iterative nature of algorithms for solving partial differential equations (PDEs) further complicate achieving convergence and efficient parallelization in real-world, non-convex problems [3]. Recent developments in fluid flow prediction have increasingly shifted toward data-driven methodologies, with deep learning-based surrogate models becoming a robust alternative to CFD simulations. These models are particularly effective in predicting complex, nonlinear fluid behavior across diverse Reynolds numbers, geometries, and flow conditions. They achieve faster convergence and enhanced computational efficiency with minimal compromise on accuracy. By leveraging sufficiently large datasets, surrogate models can recognize patterns without relying on explicit physical laws, making them particularly valuable for modeling turbulent, unsteady, or multiphase flows where traditional methods struggle. These innovations enhance fluid dynamics research and enable more sophisticated and efficient solutions for critical engineering applications [4].

The integration of data-driven surrogate models with deep learning has significantly enhanced both the precision and efficiency of fluid dynamics simulations. Nonetheless, challenges such as model generalization and the handling of high-resolution, large datasets persist, as these models must reliably predict outcomes under novel or previously unseen conditions across a diverse range of fluid flow scenarios. Achieving this level of adaptability requires sophisticated model architectures capable of accurately capturing the intricate flow dynamics observed in real-world conditions. As a result, these models often become highly complex, with millions of trainable parameters, necessitating the use of multiple GPUs to optimize training time and computational resources effectively [5].

we propose an advanced U-Net-based surrogate model specifically designed to predict complex fluid dynamics scenarios. We have employed highly optimized multi-GPU training strategies, such as DeepSpeed ZeRO, to maximize computational efficiency. The primary research goals and objectives of this work are as follows:

- Develop an advanced U-Net-based surrogate model and train it on a multi-GPU setup using data and model parallelism techniques to predict complex flow scenarios.
- Compare the performance of the U-Net model with Fourier Neural Operators when trained on a large dataset of 10,000 samples.
- Evaluate the advanced surrogate model against traditional CFD solvers by assessing convergence time, accuracy, and resource utilization, including energy consumption.

The rest of the paper is organized as follows: Section 2 explains the training data generation process and preprocessing techniques. Section 3 offers an overview of the standard U-Net model, emphasizing the enhancements in the advanced U-Net. Section 4 discusses the necessity of multi-GPU training and compares the model's results. Finally, Section 5 concludes the paper and outlines future research directions.

II. Training Data Generation:

Our study adopts a comprehensive approach to generate generalized datasets for CFD applications, emphasizing the need for geometric and positional diversity as underscored by [6]. Utilizing Python 3.8 and CadQuery 2.1, we employed a custom-developed Python script to generate a diverse array of three-dimensional shapes within a rectangular channel domain [7]. The shapes include cubes, cuboids, cones, cylinders, spheres, torus, and wedges, varying in size and orientation to create a versatile dataset suitable for a broad range of CFD studies.

To delineate regions within and around these geometries, we used signed distance functions, which provide spatial context for the geometries to the network. For simulations, we utilized the in-house developed WalBerla software, which is based on the lattice Boltzmann method (LBM) to generate true labels for supervised training. The automation script, coupled with the Fritz HPC clusters, facilitates the parallel generation of numerous simulations across multiple cores.

For data preparation, we applied rigorous preprocessing techniques, including standard scaling and min-max normalization. We observed that standard scaling was more effective for our application compared to min-max normalization. The signed distance functions will be used as inputs for the U-Net model, while the WalBerla simulations will provide the true labels for supervised learning, ensuring precise and efficient model training. In total, we have generated 10,000 training samples for extensive training of the advanced U-Net model.

For simulations, a D3Q27 lattice model, employing a cumulant collision operator, was utilized for the simulations. These simulations were conducted within a domain of size 2048 x 512 x 512. The Reynolds number was varied from 50 to 10,500.

III. Methodology

In the following section, we provide a brief overview of the standard U-Net, outlining its key components, and explore how the Advanced U-Net extends these foundations with significant enhancements.

A. U-Net

The U-Net architecture, initially designed for biomedical image segmentation, is known for its effectiveness in complex tasks due to its U-shaped structure with contracting and expanding paths [8]. It has since been enhanced and adapted, including to 3D volumes and various fields like fluid flow prediction [9], demonstrating its broad versatility and impact.

Figure 1 illustrates the standard U-Net architecture, distinguished by its unique U-shaped configuration that includes an encoder (contracting path), a bottleneck, and a decoder (expanding path). This innovative design is notable for employing an extensive number of feature channels in the upsampling section, facilitating the propagation of contextual information to higher resolution layers.

The U-Net architecture comprises three main sections: the encoder, the bottleneck, and the decoder.

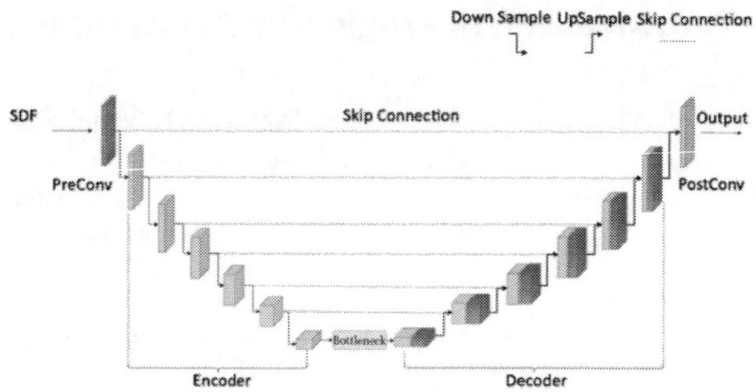

Figure 1. Schematic diagram of standard U-Net architecture

- Encoder: This initial stage, featuring convolutional layers, max pooling, activation functions, and batch normalization, reduces spatial dimensions while enhancing feature depth, and capturing critical and abstract features.
- Bottleneck: At the network's lowest resolution, the bottleneck connects the encoder and decoder, using multiple convolutional layers to handle abstracted data and integrate complex contextual information.
- Decoder: This stage reconstructs high-resolution data by increasing spatial resolution and reducing feature channels. It includes skip connections that merge upsampled outputs with encoder feature maps, reintroducing spatial details for accurate predictions.

B. Advanced U-Net Architecture and Its Component

In the following section, only the improved features over standards U-Net architecture are highlighted.

1) Repeating selected Encoder Layers without down sampling: The use of repeated encoder layers without down sampling in advanced U-Net architectures offers several significant benefits. Firstly, it enhances feature extraction by allowing the network to iteratively process and refine feature information. This iterative approach helps capture both low-level details and high-level abstractions, resulting in a more nuanced and accurate representation of the input data. Secondly, maintaining consistent spatial dimensions and input/output channels throughout these layers preserves important spatial details. This preservation is crucial for accurately representing the structure and features of the input, which is essential for tasks that require detailed spatial understanding. Additionally, the repeated encoder layers improve the network's contextual understanding by enabling it to build a more comprehensive view of complex features and relationships within the data. This leads to more precise and detailed interpretations, enhancing the overall effectiveness of the network.

2) Increasing the number of input layers and numbers of channels: Incorporating additional input layers and increasing the number of channels in a convolutional neural network significantly enhances its ability to process complex data. This increased depth enables the network to capture and analyze finer details, leading to a more sophisticated understanding of intricate features. By scaling the number of channels in encoder layers up to 2048 or even 4096, the network achieves a hierarchical feature representation. Initial layers focus on basic patterns, while deeper layers with more channels interpret these patterns in nuanced contexts, revealing detailed structures and semantic information. This hierarchical approach is particularly advantageous in applications such as high Reynolds number flows, where understanding high-frequency patterns and complex interactions is crucial.

However, expanding the network's depth and channel count introduces challenges, such as an increased risk of overfitting and higher demands on computational resources and memory during training. Managing these complexities requires careful balancing of network architecture to optimize both performance and practical feasibility.

3) Varying Kernel Sizes: The selection of kernel size is crucial in convolutional neural networks (CNNs) for effective feature extraction. Smaller kernels, such as 3x3x3, are adept at capturing fine details, such as small eddies and turbulent flow scales, which is essential for accurately predicting intricate flow scenarios. Medium-sized kernels, such as 5x5x5 and 7x7x7, strike a balance by capturing a wider range of patterns and contextual information, thereby enhancing the model's versatility. Larger kernels, like 9x9x9, are employed to cover more extensive portions of the input, enabling the identification of large-scale patterns and structural elements while maintaining global consistency in predictions. By incorporating a range of kernel sizes, CNNs can effectively capture both detailed and broad features, which is particularly advantageous for U-Net models in performing comprehensive data analysis. This varied approach enhances the network's capability to interpret complex input data across multiple scales.

4) Use of residual connection in the encoder and decoder Block: Residual connections play a crucial role in deep networks by mitigating the vanishing gradient problem, which can impede training by causing gradients to diminish through multiple layers. They preserve information by maintaining a continuous flow across layers, merging initial inputs with subsequent outputs to retain essential features. This capability enhances model convergence, as residual connections enable more effective gradient flow and faster convergence. Additionally, these connections are vital for constructing deep architectures, allowing networks to learn complex patterns without the issues typically associated with deeper models.

5) Use of advanced attentions Mechanism: Convolution Block Attention module: The Convolutional Block Attention Module (CBAM) [10] significantly enhances neural networks by focusing attention sequentially on both channel and spatial dimensions. First, the Channel Attention module compresses spatial information into a channel descriptor using global average pooling, which highlights important features and applies a ReLU activation followed by sigmoid to generate a channel attention mask. This mask refines feature importance on a channel-by-channel basis. Subsequently, the Spatial Attention module identifies critical spatial regions by pooling features across channels and combining them with a convolutional layer to create a spatial attention map, which directs the network's focus to essential areas. This dual attention mechanism enables CBAM to selectively emphasize vital features, improving the network's ability to represent complex data and enhance overall performance.

IV. Multiple GPU training of advanced U-Net model

The enhanced model iteration offers a significant improvement over the standard U-Net by incorporating additional encoder layers and expanding the number of channels, leading to enhanced feature extraction and prediction accuracy. While retaining the core methodologies of the traditional U-Net, this iteration increases both depth and analytical capability. It integrates the Convolutional Block Attention Mechanism (CBAM) and introduces residual connections within and between the encoder and decoder blocks, optimizing data processing and learning efficiency. As a result, the number of trainable parameters has increased from 80 million in the standard U-Net to 511 million in advanced U-Net, contributing to the model's complexity [11] [12].

Due to these advancements, the heightened computational demands pose challenges for training on a single GPU. The increased model complexity necessitates substantial processing power and optimal use of high-performance computing (HPC) resources. To address these challenges and enhance training efficiency, the deployment of multiple GPUs is essential. Employing PyTorch's Distributed Data Parallel (DDP) alongside DeepSpeed's ZeRO-2 [13] model parallelism strategy has facilitated effective parallel processing, resulting in a significant reduction in training time—approximately 4-5 times faster per epoch. This approach has also been instrumental in identifying the optimal resources required for training the advanced U-Net model.

A. Results and Analysis of Advanced U-Net Model:

1) Model Capacity Evaluation through Overfitting: In deep learning, particularly for complex tasks like predicting fluid velocity, assessing a model's capabilities is essential before engaging in extensive training. One effective method is to test the model's ability to overfit on a small, representative dataset. This approach helps determine if the model can accurately capture complex data patterns by minimizing loss on this subset. For evaluating a U-Net architecture, the model is deliberately overfitted on a carefully selected small dataset to drive the loss near zero compared to true labels, indicating its capability to replicate intricate details accurately. Successful overfitting, evidenced by significantly reduced loss, suggests that the model can encapsulate detailed flow dynamics. If the model fails to achieve satisfactory loss reduction, it may require architectural enhancements.

In this study, we trained both the standard and an advanced U-Net model for 500 epochs on a relatively small dataset consisting of 16 samples. The performance of the models was evaluated using the L1 loss, which measures the absolute difference between the predicted labels and the ground truth.

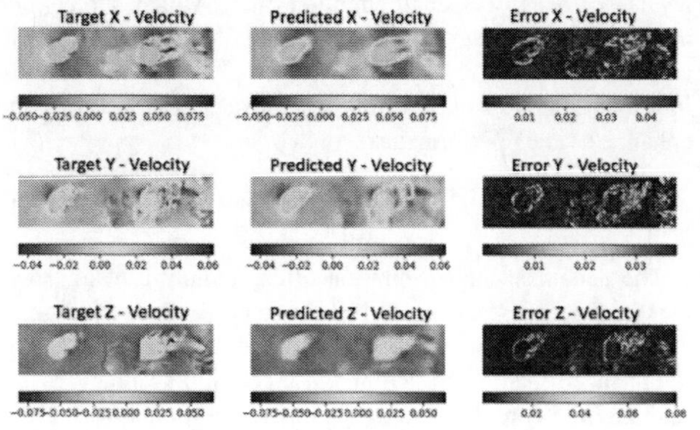

Figure 2. Comparison of Target Velocity, Predicted Velocity, and Absolute Error for each component, based on a Model trained with 16 samples for Standard U-Net Model

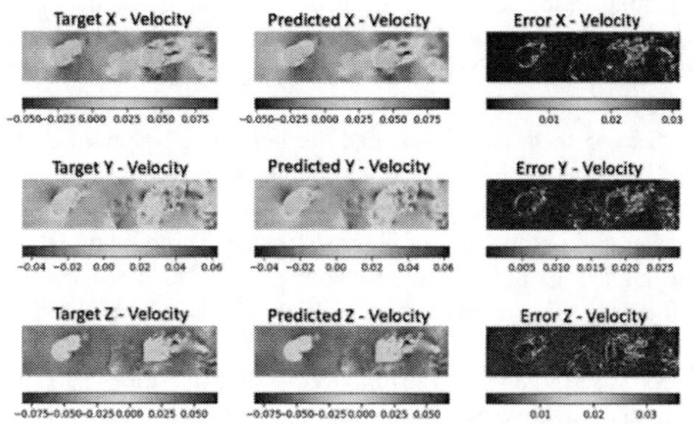

Figure 3. Comparison of Target Velocity, Predicted Velocity, and Absolute Error for each component, based on a Model trained with 16 samples for Advanced U-Net Model

The standard U-Net model yielded an L1 loss of 0.32, whereas the advanced U-Net achieved a markedly lower L1 loss of 0.09.

In terms of predictions, the standard U-Net model exhibited some resemblance to the target velocity fields but was unable to capture the finer details of the flow as seen in Figure 2. Its predictions for the X, Y, and Z velocity components appeared overly smoothed, with regions of high-velocity present but not sharply defined. For example, in the predicted X-velocity field, the regions with higher velocity values are visible, but their contours are not well defined, resulting in an oversimplified representation of the complex flow behavior. This lack of precision indicates the base model's limitations in capturing intricate velocity variations, particularly in areas where the flow is rapidly changing.

Conversely, the advanced U-Net model produced predictions that were much more aligned with the ground truth. Its predictions for the X, Y, and Z components were sharper and better represented the spatial complexity of the flow, especially in regions with high-velocity magnitudes as seen in Figure 3. Notably, the X-velocity predictions of the advanced model show a much closer match to the target, especially in areas where the flow exhibits more complex behavior. This highlights the advanced model's superior ability to capture finer details and dynamic variations in the velocity fields.

These results suggest that the modifications introduced in the advanced architecture—such as increasing the number of channels and encoder layers, as well as integrating an advanced attention mechanism—contribute significantly to its improved performance. Further evidence of the advanced U-Net's superior predictive capability is illustrated in the velocity plots comparing true labels to predictions, as presented in Figures 2 and 3.

Evaluating a model's capacity through overfitting on a small dataset effectively assesses its initial ability to predict flow with high accuracy. However, this method does not evaluate the model's performance on unseen data. Therefore, after confirming the model's capacity, it is crucial to apply regularization techniques during training on larger, more comprehensive datasets to prevent overfitting. This approach helps maintain the model's appropriate level of complexity and optimizes its effectiveness, thereby avoiding the inefficiencies associated with overly complex models. Additionally, to ensure robust performance across various flow scenarios, including both laminar and turbulent conditions, the model must be trained on an extensive dataset that encompasses all these variations. Only a sufficiently large and diverse training dataset can enable the model to learn and generalize effectively across different flow patterns.

2) Evaluation of the Advanced U-Net Model with 1000 samples: We trained both the standard U-Net and the advanced U-Net models on a relatively large dataset comprising 1,000 samples to evaluate their performance under more realistic conditions. While the standard U-Net model was able to make predictions of the velocity fields, the quality of these predictions was comparatively poor when evaluated against the advanced U-Net model as seen in Figure 4 and 5. The standard model struggled to accurately capture the flow dynamics, particularly in regions with more complex or high-velocity patterns, leading to oversimplified predictions that lacked detail and precision.

In contrast, the advanced U-Net model showed improvements in its predictive capabilities. However, its performance was still below what might be expected given its architectural advantages. Although it did not overfit the data, the predictions were not as sharp or detailed as those observed in the overfitting experiments, where the model had demonstrated the ability to perfectly capture the flow patterns on a smaller dataset. This performance gap suggests that the advanced model, while more powerful, requires further training on an even more extensive and diverse dataset to fully realize its predictive potential and generalize well to unseen data.

One of the key factors contributing to these results is that the model needs to encounter a wide range of scenarios during training in order to develop a more robust understanding of flow dynamics. With a limited number of samples, even though 1,000 represents a substantial increase over smaller datasets,

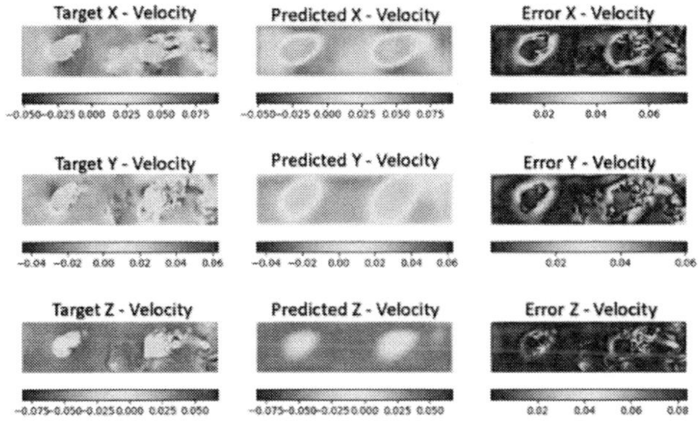

Figure 4. Comparison of Target Velocity, Predicted Velocity, and Absolute Error for each component, based on a Model trained with 800 samples and validated against 200 samples for standard U-Net Model

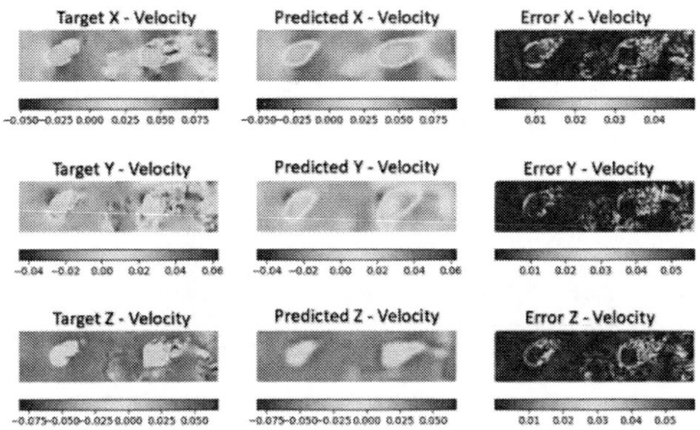

Figure 5. Comparison of Target Velocity, Predicted Velocity, and Absolute Error for each component, based on a Model trained with 800 samples and validated against 200 samples for Advanced U-Net Model

the model has not yet been exposed to all possible variations in the flow patterns. This lack of comprehensive exposure results in suboptimal generalization, especially when confronted with new, unseen data.

While the model began to learn the flow dynamics, its prediction accuracy was notably lower compared to the performance observed during the overfitting experiments. This discrepancy highlights a gap between the model's ability to fit a small dataset and its performance on a larger, more diverse set. Figure 5 illustrates the model's predictions when trained on the 1,000 samples.

V. Conclusion and Future Work

In this work, we developed an advanced U-Net architecture for fluid flow prediction in complex geometries and domains. We conducted a comparative analysis between the advanced U-Net and the standard U-Net, focusing on overfitting experiments and training performance on a dataset of 1,000 samples. The architectural improvements in the advanced U-Net enabled it to capture intricate flow patterns more effectively, resulting in a 71% improvement in overfitting performance compared to the standard U-Net. Additionally, while neither model performed as expected on the 1,000-sample dataset, the advanced U-Net demonstrated superior accuracy. These results underscore the need for further training on a larger dataset to fully realize the potential of the advanced U-Net model.

While working with the advanced U-Net model, we encountered several challenges. One significant issue is that, even though the model is adept at predicting complex fluid flows, it struggles to generalize effectively when trained on larger datasets. This difficulty underscores the importance of implementing careful and specialized training strategies to ensure accurate performance across extensive datasets.

Another issue arises when an object within a channel is relatively small, as the flow variations become concentrated around the object. In contrast, the larger portions of the channel exhibit minimal variation and are relatively simpler. This uneven distribution of flow complexity can complicate the evaluation of model performance. Specifically, using traditional loss metrics like the L1 error can produce misleading results. The L1 error might indicate a falsely reduced error if the model accurately predicts the simpler, less complex regions of the channel while failing to capture the intricate flow patterns near the object. This is because the accurate predictions in the less complex regions can overshadow the errors in the more complex regions near the object.

To mitigate this problem, one approach is to modify the error calculation by incorporating weights that emphasize the accuracy of predictions near the object. By prioritizing errors in these critical regions, this weighted error calculation helps to avoid misleadingly low error values and provides a more accurate assessment of the model's performance around complex areas.

In future we plan to extent the work with following aspects,

1) Training on a Larger Dataset: To thoroughly assess the generalization capability of the advanced U-Net model, we plan to train it on progressively larger datasets, scaling up to 10,000 samples. The aim of this step is to systematically test the model's ability to learn complex flow dynamics when exposed to a broader range of scenarios. A larger dataset will help mitigate the potential for overfitting and allow the model to generalize better to unseen cases.

In addition to this, we will conduct an ablation study to analyze the contributions of different architectural elements (e.g., the number of encoder layers, attention mechanisms, and increased channels). This will allow us to determine the importance of each feature and guide further optimization. Specifically, we will remove or alter these components one at a time to observe their direct impact on prediction accuracy, training time, and error rates. Such an approach will provide insight into which elements are critical for performance and which might be redundant or unnecessary.

2) Performance Comparison and Hybrid Model Development: We will conduct a detailed performance comparison between the advanced U-Net and the Fourier Neural Operator (FNO). The rationale behind comparing these models stems from their fundamentally different architectures: the U-Net excels in capturing local spatial features due to its convolutional nature, while the FNO is designed to efficiently model global patterns using Fourier transforms. This comparison will focus on aspects such as:

- Accuracy in capturing fine flow structures (especially in complex, high-velocity regions).
- Computational efficiency, particularly in terms of training time and resource consumption.
- Scalability with respect to dataset size and prediction time for large-scale problems.

Based on the insights from this comparison, we propose the development of a hybrid model that integrates the strengths of both architectures. The hybrid model will leverage U-Net's ability to accurately capture local features with the FNO's capacity to model large-scale, global flow dynamics. Specifically, we envision an architecture that uses U-Net layers for feature extraction at finer scales, followed by FNO layers to capture overarching patterns and relationships. This approach should improve both the accuracy and efficiency of the predictions, especially in challenging fluid dynamics simulations.

3) Evaluation of Surrogate Models: We will evaluate the performance of the surrogate model (based on the advanced U-Net or the proposed hybrid model) against traditional CFD methods. This evaluation will focus on several key performance indicators:

- Accuracy: We will measure the difference in prediction accuracy between the surrogate model and CFD simulations, focusing on both average error and maximum error in critical flow regions.
- Convergence time: Surrogate models are expected to converge much faster than conventional CFD methods. We will document and compare convergence times, particularly in simulations requiring iterative solutions over complex domains.
- Computational resources: The analysis will include detailed assessments of the computational power required by each approach, such as CPU/GPU usage, memory consumption, and overall energy expenditure. The goal is to quantify the potential cost savings of using surrogate models.

In addition, we will explore real-time applications of the surrogate model in industrial settings, where rapid simulations are often required for optimization, design iteration, or operational decision-making. The ability of the surrogate model to provide high-fidelity predictions in a fraction of the time typically required by CFD will be a significant aspect of this evaluation.

ACKNOWLEDGMENT

Innovation Study FLOWGEN has received funding through the Inno4scale project, which is funded by the European High-Performance Computing Joint Undertaking (JU) under Grant Agreement No 101118139. The JU receives support from the European Union's Horizon Europe Programme.

REFERENCES

[1] S. L. Brunton, J. N. Kutz, K Manohar, A. Y. Aravkin, K. Morgansen, J. Klemisch N. Goebel, J. Buttrick, J. Poskin, A. Blom-Schieber, T. Hogan, and D. McDonald 'Data-Driven Aerospace Engineering: Reframing the Industry with Machine Learning," ArXiv, vol.24, pp. 417-438, 2005.

[2] M. R. Bachute, and J. M. Subhedar, 'Autonomous Driving Architectures: Insights of Machine Learning and Deep Learning Algorithms," Machine Learning with Applications, vol. 6, pp.100164,issn 2666-8270, April 2024.

[3] I. I. Albarreal, M. C. Calzad, J. L. Cruz Soto and E. Fern, 'Time and space parallelization of the navier-stokes equations,"Computational & Applied Mathematics,vol 24, N. 3, pp. 417–438, 2005.

[4] O. Hiroto, and A. Takeshi, 'Prediction of steady flows passing fixed cylinders using deep learning,"Scientific Reports,vol 12, pp. 437-449, 2022.

[5] M. Telgarsky, 'Benefits of Depth in Neural Networks,"Annual Conference Computational Learning Theory, pp. 1517-1539, 2016.

[6] K. Otness, A. Gjoka, J. Bruna, D. Panozzo, B. Peherstorfer, T. Schneider, and D. Zorin, 'An Extensible Benchmark Suite for Learning to Simulate Physical Systems,"ArXiv,pp. 137-143, 2021.

[7] S. Jacob, M. Mrosek, and C. Othmer, 'Deep Learning for Real-Time Aerodynamic Evaluations of Arbitrary Vehicle Shapes,"SAE International Journal of Passenger Vehicle Systems,vol 15, pp. 77-90, March 2022.

[8] O. Ronneberger, P. Fischer, T. Brox, 'U-Net: Convolutional Networks for Biomedical Image Segmentation,"Medical Image Computing and Computer-Assisted Intervention – MICCAI ,vol 4, pp. 234-241, 2015.

[9] N. Thuerey, W. Konstantin and P. Lukas, 'Deep Learning Methods for Reynolds-Averaged Navier-Stokes Simulations of Airfoil Flows,"AIAA Journal,vol 58, pp. 25-36, 2020.

[10] S. Woo, J. Park, and J. Y. Lee, and I. S. Kweon1, 'CBAM: Convolutional Block Attention Module,"ECCV Journas, pp. 3-19, I2018.

[11] O. Hennigh, S. Narasimhan, M. A. Nabian, A. Subramaniam, and K. Tangsali , 'NVIDIA SimNet™: An AI-Accelerated Multi-Physics Simulation Framework, pp. 447-461, 2021.

[12] S. Li, Y. Zhao, R. Varma, O. Salpekar, P. Noordhuis, T. Li, A. Paszke, J. Smith, B. Vaughan, P Damania, and S. Chintala, 'PyTorch Distributed: Experiences on Accelerating Data Parallel Training,"Proceedings of the VLDB Endowment, Volume 13, Issue 12, pp. 3005-3018.

[13] S. Rajbhandari, J. Rasley, O. Ruwase, and Y. He, 'ZeRO: Memory Optimizations Toward Training Trillion Parameter Models,"ArXiv, Volume 13, Issue 12, pp. 1-16, 2020.

AI for Global Challenges: Case Studies in Urban Solar Exposure and Wildfire Management

Giorgos Filandrianos* **, Angeliki Dimitriou*, Vasiliki Kostoula*, Nikolaos Chalvantzis*, David Caballero†, Luis Torres†, Michal Kulczewski‡, Javier Cladellas§, Zoltán Horváth¶, Harald Köstler||, Konstantinos Nikas*, Dimitrios Tsoumakos*, Giorgos Stamou*

*National Technical University of Athens, Athens Greece

†MeteoGrid, Forest Fire Department Madrid, Spain

‡Poznań Supercomputing and Networking Center Poznań, Poland

§University of Strasbourg Strasbourg, France

¶Széchenyi István University Győr, Hungary

||Friedrich-Alexander-Universität Erlangen-Nürnberg Erlangen-Nürnberg, Germany

** email: geofila@islab.ntua.gr

Abstract—**Climate change poses significant challenges to environmental sustainability and human well-being, necessitating advanced tools for effective mitigation and adaptation strategies. Traditional methods for addressing issues like urban solar exposure and wildfire management often fall short due to limited predictive capabilities and inefficiencies in processing large-scale data. This paper addresses these gaps by employing Artificial Intelligence (AI) and High-Performance Data Analytics (HPDA) to enhance predictive accuracy and data handling in two critical areas: predicting shading effects between buildings for sustainable urban planning, and improving wildfire management through precomputed simulations. Our approach utilizes neural networks to model urban shading accurately and leverages HPDA to process extensive wildfire data for better preventive measures and response strategies. The main conclusion is that integrating AI and HPDA significantly enhances our ability to tackle complex climate-related challenges, providing valuable insights and tools for policymakers and urban planners.**

Keywords-AI; HPDA; Global Challenges; Urban Solar Exposure; Wildfire Management

I. Introduction

Climate change is a significant global challenge that impacts many aspects of human life and environmental health. It's evident in the increasing alterations in climate patterns across the world, affecting human health, safety, and environmental sustainability and necessitating prompt and innovative actions. The World Health Organization indicates that nearly all people globally are exposed to air quality levels that exceed safety standards, leading to about seven million deaths annually from outdoor air pollution [1]. Notably, vehicle emissions, which contribute significantly to air pollution with substances like nitrogen dioxide, account for over 40% of some harmful emissions from traffic, underscoring the need for policy and technological improvements [2][3].

The need to address global challenges is further underscored by the inefficiencies within the European Union's building sector, responsible for a substantial portion of energy use and greenhouse gas emissions. Approximately 75% of the EU's building stock is deemed energy-inefficient, presenting a critical opportunity to enhance energy performance in line with the goals of the European Green Deal [4]. Additionally, the ongoing dependence on fossil fuels intensifies these challenges, pressing the shift towards renewable energy sources like wind and solar power, which is especially crucial amidst the recent geopolitical tensions in Eastern Europe.

Moreover, global challenges extend to natural disasters, with an alarming increase in the frequency and severity of events such as wildfires and floods. Wildfires are particularly concerning, not only due to direct exposure but also because of the extensive reach of smoke pollution, which can have profound health implications on vulnerable populations across vast distances. Similarly, floods have emerged as the most frequent natural disaster, with significant human and economic losses. Modeling these phenomena numerically is an immensely complex and computationally intensive task. Computational Fluid Dynamics (CFD) [5][6][7] models, which rely on detailed three-dimensional grids and the calculations of movement within small cells, are employed. These models are highly parallelizable and scalable, making them well-suited for application on HPC architectures [8]. Despite the technological advancements, using these simulations operationally on HPC systems presents considerable challenges, including data capture, pre-processing, and computation, which can take several hours even on the most advanced systems.

This paper explores how advancements in Artificial Intelligence (AI) and High-Performance Data Analytics (HPDA) could serve as crucial tools in addressing global challenges.

More specifically, we examine how HPDA and AI can be successfully applied to two distinct use cases: assessing solar exposure in urban buildings and mitigating wildfire evolution. We will discuss how these technologies can help address related issues and provide viable solutions.

This paper is organized as follows: Section II reviews the related work. Section III introduces the formulation of the two problems investigated in this paper, namely solar exposure and wildfire management. Section IV presents the experimental results for these two use cases. Finally, Section V summarizes the conclusions of this study.

II. Related work | Methods

Artificial Intelligence (AI) has increasingly been employed to address various environmental challenges, including pollution control and renewable energy optimization. Ye et al. [9] conducted a comprehensive survey analyzing AI applications in environmental pollution control, highlighting the role of machine learning models in monitoring and predicting pollution levels. Kumar et al. [10] explored AI techniques in solar power analysis, focusing on the optimization and control of photovoltaic systems. In urban settings, AI technologies have been utilized to monitor air pollution levels, identify sources, and develop mitigation strategies [11], while machine learning models have been applied to predict future pollution trends based on historical data [12].

Despite these advancements, gaps remain in applying AI to predict urban shading effects, where traditional methods often rely on computationally intensive simulations that fail to scale or capture complex interactions effectively, hindering sustainable urban planning.

In wildfire management, traditional methods, dependent on historical and empirical data, lack the necessary spatial and temporal resolution for accurate forecasts, leading to outdated and non-responsive models [13]. Integration challenges with diverse data sources, such as weather indices and vegetation moisture levels, persist, reducing model adaptability [14]. Leveraging AI to enhance data processing and utilize real-time environmental data [15] has shown promise in improving decision-making accuracy [16][17], but computational constraints remain a significant hurdle.

The wish-list in both domains includes developing AI models capable of handling complex, large-scale data efficiently and providing accurate, real-time predictions to inform decision-making processes. Our contribution addresses these gaps by employing neural networks to predict urban shading effects, facilitating sustainable urban planning, and utilizing pre-computed wildfire simulations processed through HPDA to enhance wildfire management strategies. This approach aims to overcome current limitations by improving scalability, accuracy, and responsiveness in tackling climate-related challenges.

III. Problem Formulation

This section outlines the problem formulation for the addressed problems.

A. Solar exposure

In this use case, we investigate the dynamic interplay between urban development and solar exposure. Specifically, the focus is on understanding how shading from surrounding buildings influences the solar energy received by a target construction. Such shading effects can significantly alter temperature, humidity, and incident light levels within an area. The primary objective here is to quantify how new constructions modify solar intake and create solar masks that affect the surrounding environment. This analysis is crucial for urban planning and sustainability efforts, ensuring that new developments harmonize with their natural and built environments to optimize energy efficiency and living conditions. HPC plays a crucial role in this task, as this analysis will be conducted on a pre-calculated set of simulations of solar masks for an area before and after new construction.

B. Wildfire Management

In this use case, we explore the integration of High-Performance Computing (HPC) and Artificial Intelligence (AI) in managing severe forest fires. Simulating fires based on real-time field data is crucial for informed responses. To achieve this, we utilize a set of pre-calculated fires, employing CFD models that consider various scenarios, such as ignition points, wind speed, direction, and moisture conditions of forest fuels. These simulations could be invaluable in both designing strategies to identify vulnerable points by analyzing simulations and responding to new fires. Since simulating a new fire in real-time is impractical, we reformulate this problem as a search through a vast database of pre-computed fire simulations. Specifically, when a real-world fire is detected, its characteristics—captured through satellite or aerial imagery—are input into an AI engine that conducts a shape similarity analysis with stored simulations. This process is essential for rapidly identifying the most relevant simulations that match the current fire conditions. If no suitable matches are found, the system must swiftly compute and integrate a new simulation to aid firefighting efforts.

IV. Results

This section details findings for each problem investigated.

A. Solar exposure

To tackle the use case of predicting shading relationships between buildings, a neural network is trained using a custom dataset corresponding to the building topology of a section of Strasbourg. The dataset consists of 1,343 samples of buildings and their solar masks, accompanied by the solar masks of affected surrounding buildings which are computed in the absence of that particular building. These masks only include values that change due to the building's absence or presence. The neural network's training focuses on how solar masks evolve when new buildings are introduced, though current experiments do not consider additional factors like vegetation.

In order to predict shading relationships between buildings in a cityscape, a graph is constructed where nodes represent buildings and edges represent shading interactions. The graph

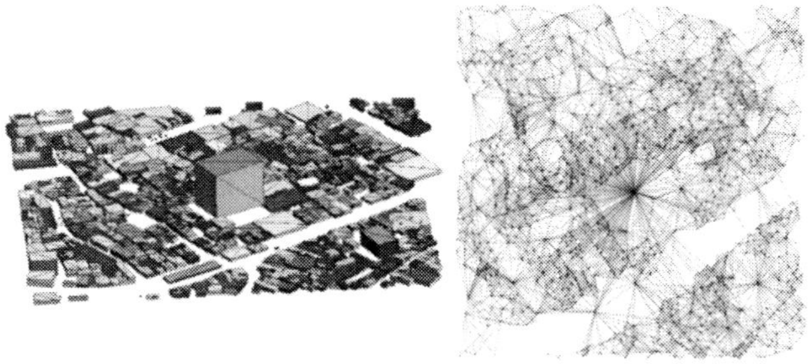

Figure 1. The affected buildings network using the proposed threshold on solar mask difference between buildings.

focuses on visualizing the topological arrangement of buildings, highlighting how they are interconnected based on their proximity and the shading they cast on each other.

The graph, termed the "affected buildings network" (Figure 1), is constructed by connecting buildings only if the removal of one affects the solar mask of another. This network can be either directed, with edges pointing toward affected buildings, or undirected. Initial observations showed that the network was dense, with edges even between distant buildings. This unexpected density was due to small changes in solar masks during dataset creation. To refine the network, a threshold was introduced: an edge is only created if the difference in solar masks, measured by the mean squared error before and after a building's deletion, is greater than or equal to 0.01, resulting in a more realistic depiction of the network.

After the creation of this graph, a transductive link prediction approach is employed to predict which structures each building shades. Link prediction involves inferring missing or potential edges between nodes in a graph. In the transductive approach, some edges are removed before training. The neural network is trained on the incomplete graph to learn patterns, and after training, it attempts to rediscover the removed edges, predicting which buildings shade each other.

The methodology employed in this study can be summarized as follows:

- **Data Preparation:** A portion of existing edges is removed while retaining all nodes (buildings). The remaining graph is then fed into a Graph Neural Network (GNN) for training.
- **Model Architecture:** A two-layer Graph Convolutional Network (GCN [18]) is utilized to encode the graph's nodes through message passing [19]. The decoder component, which performs binary classification to determine the existence of an edge between two nodes, is treated as a hyperparameter.
- **Experimental Settings:** Various experimental settings are explored, including:
  - The structure of the graph: directed vs. undirected.
  - The type of classifier: Simple Dot Product vs. Multi-Layer Perceptron (MLP).
  - Node features: Building location vs. building height.
  - The threshold on solar mask difference.

Table I reports the Area Under the Curve (AUC) for transductive Link Prediction on the affected buildings network from the initial set of experiments. This metric, commonly used in the field, measures edge classification performance. A higher ROC AUC score indicates better model performance, with a value of 1.0 representing perfect classification and 0.5 indicating a performance no better than random guessing. The table compares outcomes from two configurations: one using a threshold for solar masks and one without, allowing for a direct evaluation. Higher ROC AUC scores indicate better performance, with bolded percentages highlighting the top results in each configuration.

The initial experiments with GNN models show strong performance, with most configurations achieving high AUC scores (over 70%) even before full optimization. Early trends suggest that building location is a particularly useful feature, and undirected graphs generally perform better. Although cases with thresholded solar masks yield slightly lower AUC scores, they show better alignment with proximity, indicating promising potential for predicting affected buildings. Further optimization of the GNNs will be pursued to refine these results.

B. *Wildfires*

The core idea behind this use case is the use of a dataset of precalculated simulations for a specific area, under different scenarios. Specifically, this dataset centers on a 3x3 km^2 Wildland-Urban Interface (WUI) area in Barcelona, featuring detailed geospatial data such as Digital Terrain Models and fuel models, primarily derived from LiDAR data with 2-meter resolution. The dataset includes wind simulations for eight directions and three speeds, and 441 systematically placed initial ignition points for wildfire scenarios, culminating in a total of 10,584 simulations.

By analyzing the dataset, useful information can be extracted for informed decision-making, both in designing preventative measures against massive wildfires and in responding to new fires. For prevention, one can utilize metrics like **Burn Probability** (BP), calculated as:

$$BP = 100 \times \frac{NF}{NS} \tag{1}$$

Here, BP is the Burn Probability in percentage, NF represents the number of times fire passes through a specific point, and NS is the total number of ensemble simulations. This BP index, along with data on buildings, roads, and other vulnerable infrastructures in the area, helps assess the probability of adverse impacts. This assessment can be visualized on a risk map, as shown in Figure 2.

To make informed decisions during a new fire, it is essential to predict the fire's evolution in real time. However, conducting a new simulation under real-time conditions is unfeasible. Therefore, we propose an algorithm that employs a search mechanism on a dataset of pre-calculated simulations. Based on this dataset, the algorithm for real-time fire behavior projection is illustrated in Algorithm 3.

TABLE I. TEST AUC RESULTS FOR LINK PREDICTION (SURROUNDING AFFECTED BUILDING DISCOVERY) USING DIFFERENT HYPERPARAMETERS.

	Test AUC		Test AUC (with threshold)	
	Height	Location	Height	Location
Undirected Graph + Simple Classifier	**79.2**	**80.9**	**71.3**	71.6
Directed Graph + Simple Classifier	77.0	74.4	69.8	64.9
Undirected Graph + MLP Classifier	74.6	75.1	65.9	**78.4**
Directed Graph + MLP Classifier	71.6	74.9	55.6	77.5

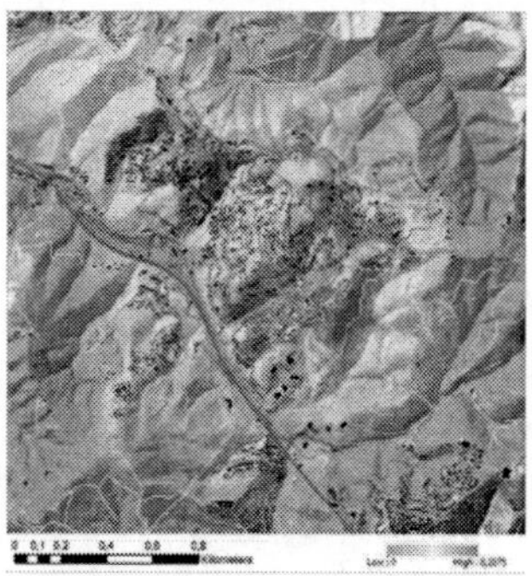

Figure 2. An example of Burn Probability (%), visualized on a map. The areas in red indicate a higher likelihood of fire spread.

Algorithm 1 Real-Time Fire Behavior Projection

Input: Fire front position captured at a specific time using satellite-borne sensors (e.g., MODIS, SUOMI, etc.)[23].
Output: Projected fire behavior based on the closest matching simulation, or a suggestion to perform a new simulation if no match is found.

Step 1: Extract the shape of the current fire front from the active (burning) areas.
Step 2: Calculate the shape descriptors for the given time.
Step 3: Consider other variables for the analysis: wind speed, wind direction, and coordinates of the point of origin (if known).
Step 4: Apply a search and discovery algorithm to a large database of simulations. The same shape descriptors and other variables are used as indexes.
Step 5: Run similarity routines to extract simulations that are closest to the observed fire front at the given time.
Step 6: Use the extracted pre-calculated simulations to project the expected fire behavior.
Step 7: If no similar simulation is found, the system suggests performing a new simulation and adding it to the database for future use.

Figure 3. The algorithm for the real-time fire behaviour prediction.

To perform similarity analysis (Steps 4 and 5), the following method is suggested for deriving basic descriptors of fire spread shapes: Extract the relevant contour from the 2D grid of the simulation, which captures fire access time at a specific point [20]. Determine the center of gravity and calculate the oriented minimum bounding box using the rotating calipers method. Identify the shape's major and minor axes, termed Length and Width, and ascertain the orientation of the major axis to indicate fire propagation direction. Finally, compute the eccentricity

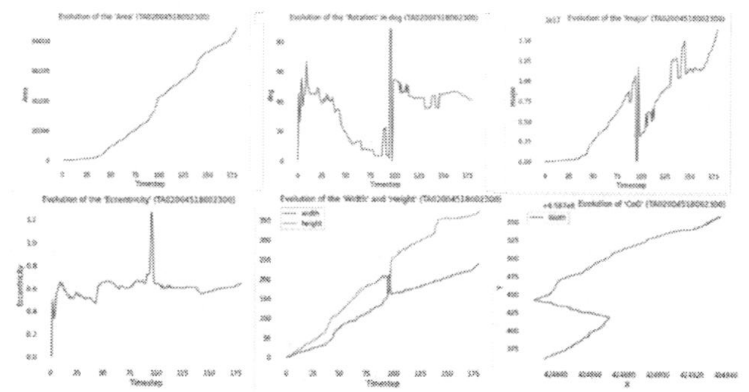

Figure 4. Illustrates the evolution of the six features: "Area," "Rotation," "Imajor," "Eccentricity," "Width," "Height," and "Center of Gravity of the contour" for each timestep.

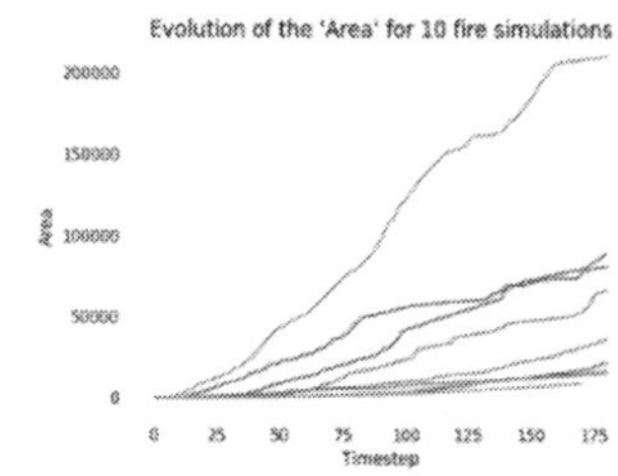

Figure 5. The evolution of the "Area" feature across ten different forest fires.

(length-to-width ratio) and the moment of inertia relative to the major axis. Additional shape descriptors proposed for use in similarity analysis include the total area enclosed by the shape, the total length of the shape's perimeter, its eccentricity, orientation angle, and moment of inertia.

Figures 4 illustrate the evolution of features during a single fire, aimed at evaluating the effectiveness of handcrafted features in capturing fire progression. Figure 5 depicts the "Area" feature across 10 different fire simulations, revealing varying rates of fire spread—some expand rapidly, while others progress more slowly. This comparison highlights the diverse behaviors of wildfires under different conditions.

The distinct trajectories of handcrafted shape descriptors across these fires demonstrate that each fire follows a unique path. While this uniqueness aids in identifying a fire's progression based on these features, it complicates locating similar fire simulations for new fires. To further explore this uniqueness,

Principal Component Analysis (PCA) was applied to reduce the dimensionality of the fire data for visualization. Figure 6 shows the PCA results: the left panel displays PCA features color-coded by fire simulation filenames, while the right panel color-codes them by the timestep from which each vector was extracted. The fire data follows a consistent linear trajectory, indicating close relationships between features at each timestep. However, the lower and central parts of the diagram reveal a distinct cluster of blue points at timestep zero (as shown in the right panel where blue points correspond to the positions at timestep zero), seemingly unrelated to the rest of the fire's evolution. This poses a challenge in identifying similar wildfires when only early-stage data is available.

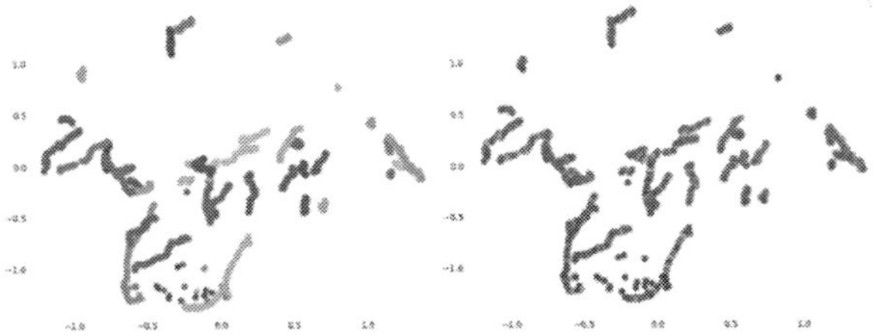

Figure 6. The results of PCA for each timestep of fire simulation.

In this pipeline, user preferences dictate the search algorithm and its features. The key contribution is showing how pre-calculated simulations facilitate proactive and reactive wildfire management.

V. Conclusion and Future Work

This study explores approaches for two distinct challenges—predicting solar shading effects and managing wildfires—using AI and HPC. Corresponding tools effectively correlate shading relations between buildings through characteristics like building proximity and height, or respectively aid in designing preventive measures against wildfires by analyzing the Burn Probability (BP) and supporting rapid response strategies by matching real-time fire scenarios with pre-calculated simulations. For wildfires, the next steps include testing various similarity algorithms and enhancing accuracy with visual features, terrain data, and multimodal inputs. For solar exposure, the focus will be on tuning GNNs, node features, and exploring shading mask evolution over time.

Acknowledgment

This work has been developed as part of the HiDALGO2 project, which has received funding from the European High Performance Computing Joint Undertaking (JU) and Poland, Germany, Spain, Hungary, France and Greece under grant agreement No 101093457.

References

[1] World Health Organization, *Billions of people still breathe unhealthy air: New who data*, https://www.who.int/news/item/04-04-2022-billions-of-people-still-breathe-unhealthy-air-new-who-data, Accessed: 29/08/2024, Apr. 2022.

[2] Our World in Data, *Who air pollution deaths*, https://ourworldindata.org/data-review-air-pollution-deaths, Accessed: 29/08/2024, 2022.

[3] The Local, *Eu planning to sue germany over dirty air in cities*, https://www.thelocal.com/20171115/eu-planning-to-sue-germany-over-dirty-air-in-cities-report/, Accessed: 29/08/2024, Nov. 2017.

[4] European Commission, *Focus on energy efficiency in buildings*, https://commission.europa.eu/news/focus-energy-efficiency-buildings-2020-02-17_en, Accessed: date-of-access, Feb. 2020.

[5] T. Chung, *Computational fluid dynamics*. Cambridge university press, 2002.

[6] K. McGrattan, "Progress in modeling wildland fires using computational fluid dynamics", in *Proceedings of the 10th US National Combustion Meeting, College Park, MD, USA*, 2017, pp. 23–26.

[7] S. Haider, A. Paquier, R. Morel, and J.-Y. Champagne, "Urban flood modelling using computational fluid dynamics", in *Proceedings of the Institution of Civil Engineers-Water and Maritime Engineering*, Thomas Telford Ltd, vol. 156, 2003, pp. 129–135.

[8] S. Jamshed, *Using HPC for Computational Fluid Dynamics: A guide to high performance computing for CFD engineers*. Academic Press, 2015.

[9] Z. Ye *et al.*, "Tackling environmental challenges in pollution controls using artificial intelligence: A review", *Science of The Total Environment*, vol. 699, p. 134 279, 2020, ISSN: 0048-9697. DOI: https://doi.org/10.1016/j.scitotenv.2019.134279.

[10] A. Kumar, A. K. Dubey, I. Segovia Ramírez, A. Muñoz del Río, and F. P. García Márquez, "Artificial intelligence techniques for the photovoltaic system: A systematic review and analysis for evaluation and benchmarking", *Archives of Computational Methods in Engineering*, pp. 1–25, 2024.

[11] S. Subramaniam *et al.*, "Artificial intelligence technologies for forecasting air pollution and human health: A narrative review", *Sustainability*, vol. 14, no. 16, p. 9951, 2022.

[12] T. G. Krupnova, O. V. Rakova, K. A. Bondarenko, and V. D. Tretyakova, "Environmental justice and the use of artificial intelligence in urban air pollution monitoring", *Big Data and Cognitive Computing*, vol. 6, no. 3, p. 75, 2022.

[13] J. Zhou, W. Jiang, F. Wang, Y. Qiao, and Q. Meng, "Comparing accuracy of wildfire spread prediction models under different data deficiency conditions", *Fire*, vol. 7, no. 4, p. 141, 2024.

[14] A. Jadouli and C. E. Amrani, *Enhancing wildfire forecasting through multisource spatio-temporal data, deep learning, ensemble models and transfer learning*, 2024. arXiv: 2407.15878 [cs.LG].

[15] R. Kanwal, W. Rafaqat, M. Iqbal, and S. Weiguo, "Data-driven approaches for wildfire mapping and prediction assessment using a convolutional neural network (cnn)", *Remote Sensing*, vol. 15, no. 21, p. 5099, 2023.

[16] P. Jain *et al.*, "A review of machine learning applications in wildfire science and management", *Environmental Reviews*, vol. 28, no. 4, pp. 478–505, 2020.

[17] M. Feldman, "Intelligence versus inferno: How artificial intelligence can be used to monitor and manage wildfires in europe", 2023.

[18] T. N. Kipf and M. Welling, "Semi-supervised classification with graph convolutional networks", *arXiv preprint arXiv:1609.02907*, 2016.

[19] J. Gilmer, S. S. Schoenholz, P. F. Riley, O. Vinyals, and G. E. Dahl, "Message passing neural networks", *Machine learning meets quantum physics*, pp. 199–214, 2020.

[20] M. Marengoni and D. Stringhini, "High level computer vision using opencv", in *2011 24th SIBGRAPI Conference on Graphics, Patterns, and Images Tutorials*, IEEE, 2011, pp. 11–24.

Cybersecurity Concerns of Artificial Intelligence Applications on High-Performance Computing Systems

Rishabh Saxena, Aadesh Baskar, Sameer Haroon,
Sameed Hayat, Oleksandr Shcherbakov, Kerem Kayabay, Dennis Hoppe
High-Performance Computing Center Stuttgart (HLRS)
University of Stuttgart
Stuttgart, Germany
e-mail: {firstname.lastname}@hlrs.de

Abstract—**The High-Performance Computing (HPC) landscape is undergoing profound changes with developments in fast-growing domains such as Artificial Intelligence (AI), cloud, edge computing, and quantum computing. The growth of AI has particularly impacted the relatively isolated HPC realm, bringing in new user communities like start-ups that don't want to fall behind and are increasingly dependent on foundational models trained by a handful of companies. However, the rapidly growing AI technology landscape introduces security vulnerabilities to the HPC world, which hesitates to install and maintain potentially unstable software. This paper is a first step towards enabling secure AI workloads on HPC systems by investigating AI security vulnerabilities using the AI Lifecycle. We then organize the challenges for HPC centres through the lens of the Technology-Organization-Environment (TOE) framework. Lastly, we discuss the differences between AI security concerns and mitigation strategies on HPC and other systems, and outline future work towards secure AI workloads on HPC systems.**

Keywords-High-Performance Computing (HPC), Artificial Intelligence (AI), AI Security Vulnerabilities, TOE Framework

I. INTRODUCTION

Supercomputers are the fastest computers of their time, and have long been geared towards solving complex, time-intensive problems. As Strohmaier *et al.* [1] notes, the traditional focus on floating-point intensive technical applications is no longer sufficient to survive in the market. The HPC landscape is undergoing profound changes with the emergence of Machine Learning (ML) and Deep Learning (DL), cloud and edge computing, and quantum computing. This paper looks at the growth of AI and the need for HPC to embrace these technologies and attract new user communities while ensuring a high level of security. This is crucial to remain an attractive computing platform for Small and Medium-Sized Enterprise (SMEs), start-ups, and industry.

Why is the growth in AI relevant for supercomputing? There are actually two sides to the coin: First, AI needs the processing power of HPC, which is, after tackling technical barriers, a straightforward task. Second, HPC should leverage AI to improve classical simulations and system operation. This task is quite challenging because it predominantly requires expertise in both, AI and HPC.

Updating most of today's HPC systems to support AI workflows is a challenge, as it opens up the relatively isolated HPC realm, bringing it out of its secure bubble to a higher, and still relatively unknown, level of security risks. Moreover, many HPC system administrators focus on traditional HPC application areas like engineering and chemistry, which makes it difficult for them to fully understand the specific needs of emerging user communities, such as those in AI. This is especially true for widely used AI frameworks (e.g., TensorFlow and PyTorch) that are part of the rapidly evolving ecosystem of AI software and libraries, and are in stark contrast to the limited legacy software that administrators maintain on traditional HPC systems, over which they have much greater control and experience. Therefore, there is some resistance in installing and maintaining software from the AI realm that is potentially unstable or may have security vulnerabilities, as well as allowing such software to train and execute potentially malicious or exploitable AI models.

Nevertheless, ways must be found to enable AI workloads on HPC systems. If not, there is a growing risk that the academic world, along with start-ups and SMEs, will continue to fall behind and become increasingly dependent on the foundational models, or their powered-down versions, provided by bigger companies [2]. It is not possible for SMEs to build up and train their own counterparts to foundational models, without access to federal or academic supercomputing resources. To this end, HPC experts and AI experts must jointly develop solutions that allow using pure AI applications and workflows on HPC and thus enabling seamless, hybrid HPC/AI workflows. The technical obstacles include, for example, making the entire AI software stack available for HPC systems (e.g., via containerisation), evaluating AI-specific usage patterns, and cybersecurity aspects. This paper focuses on the cybersecurity concerns for running large-scale AI applications on HPC systems.

In order to acquaint the reader with the foundations, the paper first leads into a quick review of each of the main concepts, namely, HPC, AI on HPC, and cybersecurity on HPC. Then a thorough investigation is carried out on the technical areas of concern that threaten or undermine the usage of ML workflows on HPC, followed by potential challenges at an organisational level for HPC centres, through the lens of the TOE framework [3]. Finally, we review the potential problems and solutions presented in the paper, and discuss how our findings relate to research in the state of the art, and what future work could lead on from this paper.

II. Literature Review

The literature review explores the role of HPC systems, their integration with AI, and cybersecurity considerations, while identifying related work and existing knowledge gaps.

A. HPC

1) The Importance of HPC for Diverse User Communities: HPC is utilized across industry [4] and academia, with use cases as diverse as simulating fluid flows in the turbulence around aeroplanes to the fluid flow of blood through the human heart [5], from carrying out genome sequencing in biology to molecular simulations in nuclear fusion [6], and from predictions ranging from weather forecasts, financial markets, and the spread of diseases and pandemics [7] [8]. Most of these diverse use cases can be classified into two basic classes of problems, tracking and simulating the interactions of a large system of individual particles, and solving forms of partial differential equations. Often, solving these problems results in solving a Linear Algebraic system [9].

2) An overview of an HPC system: A supercomputer, or HPC cluster, derives its processing power from aggregating and coordinating huge number of individual computational systems. It not only orchestrates the parallel execution of users' programs, called codes, over these systems, but also handles many users and their codes simultaneously [9]. These individual systems, or nodes, of an HPC system vary according to their tasks. Login nodes provide initial access to the system, as well as basic storage and standardised interfaces, such as to the scheduling system (sometimes running on dedicated scheduler or head nodes) [10]. The Scheduler allocates users the access to compute (or worker) nodes. These are resource heavy nodes equipped to do the heavy lifting of executing application codes, and themselves come in different flavours, such as pure Central Processing Unit (CPU) nodes, mixed CPU and Graphics Processing Unit (GPU) nodes, pure General-Purpose Graphics Processing Unit (GPGPU) nodes, and data transfer nodes [11]. All the nodes making up an HPC cluster use a choice of high-performance interconnect to distribute data and instructions amongst themselves, such as InfiniBand or Gigabit Ethernet [12].

The user must design their program keeping in mind the parallel architecture of a supercomputer, from the level of multiple cores in a single processor, to multiple processors in a single node, and finally scaling up to the nodes required or available on the HPC system [11]. The design of the program must also understand and make use of the memory architecture of the system, with hybrid models of shared memory and distributed memory paradigms available on most HPC systems. Ultimately, it is the design of the application code, including the exploitation of parallel frameworks such as Message Passing Interface (MPI) and Open Multi-Processing (OpenMP), that determines how efficiently it can harness the power of the HPC system [13].

B. AI on HPC

The rise in the level of AI model complexity and size to exponential levels poses an unprecedented computational requirement, thus the adoption of HPC resources [14] [15]. Modern AI models, especially Large Language Models (LLMs), contain hundreds of billions of parameters that far exceed the memory capacity of a single GPU [15] [16]. This growth, coupled with expansion in training datasets, creates a number of technical challenges that only HPC is well-poised to tackle.

The driving technical requirements of AI's need for HPC are many. First, the model size already far exceeds single GPU memory capability and requires distributed computing approaches [16] [17]. Second, very large data sets already used for training exceed single machine memory and storage capability [14] [17]. Third, this computational intensity of training resulted in prohibitively long training times on conventional hardware [16] [17].

Moreover, research on AI does require long hyperparameter tuning and thus many training runs with different settings are needed. HPC clusters, therefore, provide the best environment for these parallel experiments due to their high functionality in job scheduling and resource management systems [16] [17].

The high computational demands of AI are challenging existing computing platforms. AI workloads are already driving the architecture of new HPC hardware, particularly in the construction of higher-end, more powerful, and more efficient GPUs and dedicated AI accelerators [16] [17]. Software frameworks evolve to better cope with distributed AI training and inference on HPC clusters, with innovation in techniques such as model parallelism and pipeline parallelism [16] [17]. This convergence pushes the frontiers of both AI and HPC to handle the ever-increasing scale and complexity of AI models and datasets [18], also raising significant concerns, such as cybersecurity.

C. Cybersecurity on HPC

Similar to the general purpose Information Technology (IT) systems, HPC systems face a variety of threats that can affect their confidentiality, integrity, and availability. Some examples are stealing of compute cycles, unauthorized access, Denial of Service (DoS), data breaches and leakage, misuse of compute power, and alteration of code. When comparing HPC with general purpose IT systems, there are differences in their functions, software and hardware stack, the user community and the workflow.

Peisert [19] considers these differences and presents the challenges and opportunities in implementing cybersecurity for HPC. A single ingress and egress point between the cluster and the external world makes it easy to monitor and restrict the traffic. Not all nodes in the cluster are directly accessible by the users. The users connect to the login nodes to submit the jobs and data transfer nodes to pull the data from external sources. The login nodes and data transfer nodes are placed behind firewalls or protected by Access Control Lists in the routers or switches. They might be accessible only through secure protocols like SSH for login and GridFTP for data transfer [20].

The compute nodes can only be used by submitting a job to the resource manager and are not directly accessible by

TABLE I: AI VULNERABILITIES IN SECONDARY STUDIES

Study	Identified Vulnerabilities
Huq *et al.* [26]	Training data poisoning, trojaning, LeftOverLocals
Familoni [27]	Adversarial attacks, data breaches, deepfakes, distributed DoS, phishing, cyber conflicts, evolving malware, data poisoning
Roshanaei *et al.* [28]	Adversarial attacks, data poisoning, model stealing, model inversion, infrastructure attacks
Blowers and Williams [29]	Steganographic attack, evolving malware, deep fakes
Kaloudi and Li [30]	Evasive malware, evolving malware, voice synthesis, social bots, adversarial training
Muñoz-González and Lupu [31]	Data poisoning, exploratory attacks, evasive attacks, availability violation, data stealing
Hu *et al.* [32]	Data breach, data biases/fake data, sensor spoofing attack, image scaling attack, data poisoning attack, adversarial attacks, availability attack, data stealing, model stealing, AI framework backdoors

the user. The resource manager that allocates the nodes and schedules the jobs can use its own authentication mechanism. A simple example of such an authentication mechanism is Munge used by Slurm to encode the user credentials of a calling process and decode them in a remote node [21]. Multi-tenancy in HPC enables jobs from multiple users to run at the same time in the cluster. Even if a given node remains exclusive to a particular user's job, all the nodes in the cluster will be connected to the same network. Prout *et al.* [22] offers a solution for this problem by implementing network policies based on user and group IDs of the application processes. Since the HPC providers can support users from various institutions and SMEs in the same cluster, the need for proper configuration of file-system access control is crucial. Discretionary Access Control is configured by the owners of the file to restrict permissions to their file and Mandatory Access Control is configured by the system administrators [23].

Since the primary goal of HPC systems is to offer very high compute power, the overheads from security tools are not acceptable. This presents a challenge in directly using security tools available from the general-purpose web/software development ecosystem. However, the world of HPC is witnessing serious change due to requirements emerging from diverse user communities. One such trend is the increased adoption of containers that provide reproducibility, flexibility, and portability in shipping applications. The usage of containers can provide extra attack surface and can be risky in multi-tenant HPC clusters [24]. Keller Tesser and Borin [25] stress on the importance of unprivileged user containers to reduce the risks associated with using containers in multi-tenant systems. The following sections review such vulnerabilities, focusing on the AI domain's requirements.

D. Related Work and Gaps

Before discussing the cybersecurity concerns of large-scale AI applications on HPC systems, we should discuss the secondary studies with similar objectives (Table I). Huq *et al.* [26] survey the cloud-based GPU threats and their impact on AI, HPC, and Cloud Computing. The report explores potential attacks against AI using GPUs. Familoni [27] reviews the cybersecurity concerns in AI systems. After presenting the vulnerabilities, the paper points out the challenges in securing AI systems, including human factors and the lack of explainability and transparency in AI systems. Roshanaei *et al.* [28] identify the defensive mechanisms and frameworks after specifying the potential threats to AI systems. Following an introduction to potential vulnerabilities, Blowers and Williams [29] emphasize the design considerations for secure AI/ML architectures. Kaloudi and Li [30] focus on the intentional use of AI for harmful purposes, classifying the attack stages and objectives in a cyber threat framework with defensive approaches. Muñoz-González and Lupu [31] introduce a threat model that organizes the ML vulnerabilities by attacker's capability, goal, and knowledge. Hu *et al.* [32] map the attacks on AI systems to the AI lifecycle comprising data collection, data preprocessing, training, inference, and integration phases.

As AI systems become larger, driven by competition among a handful of large companies, it is critical that start-ups and SMEs also have access to the computational power needed to train and deploy foundational models [33]. Furthermore, researchers also need the computational capability to evaluate these large models [34]. Therefore, we need secure HPC infrastructures to train, evaluate, and deploy large-scale AI systems. To the best of our knowledge, the literature lacks studies that organize large-scale AI vulnerabilities into an ML lifecycle framework from the HPC perspective, and map the challenges HPC centres face in solving AI system vulnerabilities. The next section organizes large-scale AI system vulnerabilities on HPC and classifies the challenges for HPC centres.

III. AI CYBERSECURITY FOR HPC SYSTEMS

This section examines the cybersecurity risks in the ML lifecycle on HPC systems and the challenges of addressing AI vulnerabilities using the TOE framework.

A. Potential Risks in the ML Lifecycle on HPC

Since the ML lifecycle involves multiple steps and use-cases, multiple points of attack can be exploited by potential bad actors. This subsection briefly details a non-exhaustive list of security risks associated with ML pipelines, with an emphasis on how HPC is particularly exposed to such risks.

- **Problem Definition**: The first vulnerability that must be addressed, even before looking into technical security risks, is that of the usage of HPC resources for malicious use-cases or ill-posed applications. Blauth et al. [35] mention various categories of malicious uses of AI, such as social engineering models, misinformation and fake news, hacking, and warfare-related AI. These risks are significant because detecting the development of these models requires manual oversight. This necessitates a more stringent review of projects and code on HPC systems at computing centres, along with periodic checks to ensure only relevant tasks are performed.
- **Data Exploration**: Development of ML systems usually begins with an Exploratory Data Analysis (EDA) phase [36],

where the users and developers understand the composition of the data and problem that needs to be solved. Since HPC is a component of the pipeline, and not the only available infrastructure during the development lifecycle, most ML development takes place in a heterogeneous computing environment [37]. In such scenarios, a mixture of traditional HPC, cloud, and edge computing is used to distribute different phases of the lifecycle. Because EDA is an iterative and experimental phase, it often requires developers to connect their local systems to HPC or cloud systems outside the normal job-based scheduling environment. With the steady increase in model size and training requirements [38], HPC environments have become more relevant for EDA.
Security risks during EDA on cloud systems has also become equally relevant [39], and as such, also extends to the HPC environment. Since EDA on HPC requires opening ports to the outside world, this presents a unique challenge where security vulnerabilities throughout the chain of connections may affect the source HPC system. Where most cloud providers deploy their EDA environments through containerization, these methods become difficult to implement in a batch-scheduling system. The most famous containerization engine, Docker, requires root-access, which presents a security risk when provided within a shared, HPC environment. On the other hand, development of rootless containers, such as Singularity/Apptainer [40], are not well integrated with other systems. We further discuss the security issues with container runtimes in HPC environments in the next section, under technological challenges. As such, EDA on HPC systems is usually more time-consuming task, in order to maintain security.

- **Data Ingestion**: Similar to providing an environment for EDA, HPC infrastructure must also allow for transportation and ingestion of vast amounts of data, especially for AI/ML development. This risk is mitigated in the cloud using encryption at rest, transmission and source, along with lifecycle features. Since most ML development in the cloud uses object storage [41], this differs from the traditional HPC approach. Connecting these systems is challenging because higher bandwidth data transmission requires multiple steps between the source and destination, increasing vulnerabilities [42], [43], including man-in-the-middle attacks [44].
- **Data Engineering**: Even when the data can be securely moved around different storage resources throughout the pipeline, further risks exists that can be exploited by bad actors. Once the data is at rest, engineering and utilizing this data for further processing becomes even more important. Kumar et al. [45] show that there are various security risks involved with data pipelines, specifically in cloud systems, such as risks involving confidentiality (access to the data), integrity (tampering with the data), availability (DoS), risks involving authentication and access-control (since most cloud data pipelines are built with a singular authentication mechanism), and other minor risks such as data location, multi-tenancy and backup of data. These risks also extend to HPC storage systems, where the storage system must also deal with these security risks. Adversarial attacks via malicious actors, such as poisoning attacks [46] can cause loss of data integrity, both for cloud and HPC systems.
- **Model Training**: Another attack vector is the training and code execution of models. ML pipelines either train a model from scratch using multiple libraries, such as TensorFlow, PyTorch, and Scikit-learn. Although these libraries have active development teams to patch discovered vulnerabilities, they still possess a variety of security risks. [47]. When these libraries are used to train a model, there may be open back-doors that allow bad actors to execute malicious code. Apart from pre-training models, pre-trained models hosted on various repositories may also contain malicious code embedded into the model file itself, such as backdoor code, weight poisoning attacks, and falsified model description [48]. Although root privileges are generally unavailable on HPC systems, any cloud-HPC ML pipeline may have privileged steps that allow such spillover.
- **Model Evaluation**: Another major step in the ML pipeline is the evaluation of pre-trained models. In this step, the developers usually look at evaluating the model against a test or live dataset, and predict the performance of such models. Major security issues posed during this step are evasion attacks and model inversion attacks [46], where the bad actor might poison the dataset for evaluation, in order to falsify the final output, or simply switch the model output entirely. These attacks can cause falsified information to be used when using these models in the real world. This is a particularly difficult problem within the HPC environment since HPC resources are expensive, and falsified evaluation results from ML training may cause excessive usage of resources.
- **Model Deployment**: Toward the end of an ML pipeline, before monitoring and maintenance, is usually the deployment of the model in a production environment. Here, the usual security risks of any cloud environment [45] become automatically relevant. Apart from these, model ML specific attacks that are relevant at these steps are surveyed by Chen et al. [49], where they mention attacks such as distributed DoS attacks on deployed models, model inversion and extraction attacks (where the output of the model is used to replicate the model by prompting it with different datasets), membership inversion attacks [46] (where the attacker can generate the underlying dataset of the model, along with other parameters, by repeatedly querying the model), as well as injecting malicious code during batch inferencing of ML models. There may be threats present if any attacker gains access to a GPU session, even after the GPU session has ended, by extracting the information execution on GPUs [26]. In case these models are being hosted within the HPC environment, this may lead to a loss of confidential information and other secrets. Lastly, as models get larger and more complex, it becomes harder and more computationally expensive to thoroughly evaluate them before deploying to production. Large-scale models bring many opportunities, but additional care is necessary

for critical domains such as law [2].

- **Monitoring and Maintenance**: The production ML models are usually ephemeral because the model performance degrades over time [50]. Continuous Integration (CI) and Continuous Delivery (CD) have increasingly become prominent methodologies to automate software development in the industrial landscape, as well in the HPC/AI domain. This is because CI/CD plays an important role in automated monitoring to track the model performance in real-time, automated retraining, and rollbacks. Since CI/CD require multiple components, such as a central version control repository like Git, and execution platforms such as runners, there are multiple vectors of attack available for bad actors. To encapsulate this pipeline, most CI/CD tools use Docker containers, which come with their own vulnerabilities [51] such as insecure configurations, privilege escalation, and changing of container permissions through exploits. Apart from this, other vulnerabilities, such as running malicious code within the CI/CD pipeline is another risk factor, which is compounded when HPC is involved as a component in the pipeline. If the initial code being tested and built is compromised, the privilege provided to the runners might spill over the infection to the HPC system, thereby creating a security issue for the entire-cluster.

In the next subsection, we will look at why these risks are difficult to solve, even when they may be known.

B. Challenges in Addressing AI Vulnerabilities on HPC

To address AI vulnerabilities on HPC, we use the TOE framework [3], which explains how three contextual factors—technology, organization, and environment—affect an organization's adoption and implementation of innovations.

1) Technological challenges: While AI applications bring immense potential to HPC environments, integrating these innovations introduces several technological challenges.

- **Increasing Spectrum of Hardware Components**: Modern HPC systems are incorporating a growing variety of hardware components to enhance computational power, energy efficiency, and specialized processing capabilities. These components can range from traditional CPUs and GPUs to more specialized hardware like Tensor Processing Units (TPUs) and even quantum processors. The inclusion of such diverse and sometimes exotic hardware increases the complexity of managing security across the entire HPC environment. Each type of hardware component in an HPC system may have unique security requirements. For instance, GPUs and TPUs optimized for parallel processing might have different memory management vulnerabilities compared to CPUs. Exotic and cutting-edge hardware components in HPC systems may have unique firmware and micro-architectural vulnerabilities that are less well understood or documented. Attackers can exploit these low-level vulnerabilities through techniques like side-channel attacks (exploit information gained from the physical implementation of a computer system rather than vulnerabilities in the code itself [52]), row hammer attacks [53] (hardware vulnerability in DRAM memory), or Spectre [54], and Meltdown-type [55] exploits (exploit speculative execution - a performance optimization in modern CPUs - to access unauthorized memory). The challenge is to ensure robust and properly managed security configurations for each hardware type. This includes avoiding conflicts or vulnerabilities and consistently identifying, patching, and protecting against vulnerabilities on various devices, often requiring specialized knowledge.
- **Performance-Security Trade-offs**: HPC applications are designed to maximize performance, as the scalability of these systems means that any performance loss also scales significantly. Consequently, HPC users value security measures only when they come with a tolerable performance penalty [24]. To achieve optimal performance, HPC systems often operate as shared environments where multiple tenants can access shared resources, such as access nodes and certain network layers. This is in contrast to cloud systems, which are predominantly virtualized. In cloud environments, each tenant or user has isolated virtualized compute and network resources, reducing the risk of cross-tenant interference or data leakage.
- **Evolution of AI, Big Data, and HPC Software Ecosystems**: AI, Big Data, and HPC have evolved within distinct software ecosystems, each optimized for different goals and environments. AI software ecosystems are built around cloud-native, containerized environments with frameworks like TensorFlow, PyTorch, and Keras. Big Data ecosystems, such as Apache Hadoop and Spark, are designed for distributed storage and processing of vast datasets. Meanwhile, supercomputer ecosystems focus on HPC with specialized libraries and frameworks like MPI and OpenMP optimized for parallel processing. The divergence in software ecosystems creates significant challenges when integrating AI and Big Data workflows with HPC environments. The AI and Big Data frameworks often lack the native compatibility with HPC-specific software and libraries. Managing dependencies and ensuring version compatibility across these ecosystems is a non-trivial task. AI and Big Data frameworks evolve rapidly with frequent updates and new releases, whereas HPC software stacks may rely on more stable, tested versions. Ensuring compatibility between different versions, libraries, and tools without exposing the system to vulnerabilities or performance issues is a considerable challenge.
- **Cloud-Native ML Frameworks and HPC Security Compatibility**: The distributed ML libraries and frameworks, such as TensorFlow, PyTorch, Horovod or Ray, have been developed primarily with cloud infrastructure assumptions in mind. However, these frameworks rely on the inherent isolation provided by cloud virtualization for security and require users to manage infrastructure-level security settings [56]. In an HPC environment, where such virtualized isolation is often absent, deploying these frameworks securely becomes challenging. The lack of compatibility with HPC security requirements means these frameworks may inadvertently

expose vulnerabilities when deployed in non-virtualized environments. This creates a challenge of either adapting these frameworks or fundamentally redesigning the HPC environment to support them securely.

- **Maturity of Distributed ML Libraries and Frameworks:** As mentioned above, distributed ML libraries and frameworks are still in relatively early stages of their development lifecycle, tending to prioritize performance and scalability over security, and leading to a lack of robust built-in security features. For example, they may not have mature mechanisms for handling control or secure communication, which are critical in multi-tenant HPC environments. This creates vulnerabilities that could be exploited in environments where sensitive data is processed. They may also focus heavily on performance optimization and may employ shortcuts or assumptions that do not hold in more secure or controlled environments like HPC. For instance, assuming trusted environments and thus lacking robust isolation between processes, increases the risk of side-channel attacks or data leakage.
- **Security Issues with Container Runtimes in HPC Environments**: Most container runtimes (software responsible for running containers, managing container images, and providing necessary tools and libraries to support containerized applications), such as Docker, traditionally require root (administrator) privileges to manage containers, which poses a significant security risk in HPC environments. Running containers with root privileges can lead to a potential exploitation where malicious users can gain unauthorized access to the underlying host system. This is particularly concerning in multi-tenant HPC setups, where ensuring isolation and security between different users and their workloads is crucial. HPC-oriented container runtimes like Apptainer (formerly Singularity) and Podman are designed to address some of these security concerns by allowing containers to run in a "rootless" mode, which avoids requiring root privileges. However, these runtimes rely heavily on user namespaces (a Linux kernel feature that allows a process and its children to have a different view of the system's user and group IDs; this enables root privileges within the namespace without granting those privileges on the host system) to provide isolated environments. Recent history has shown that user namespaces have been subject to vulnerabilities, such as CVE-2022-0492, CVE-2022-0185, CVE-2021-22555 where a flaw in the user namespace handling could lead to privilege escalation. Such vulnerabilities undermine the security guarantees provided by rootless containerization in HPC environments. Alternatively, udocker [57] is a unique container runtime that operates entirely in user space, meaning it does not require root or system-level privileges to execute. This design significantly reduces the risk of privilege escalation attacks, a common concern with other containerization tools that rely on elevated privileges. Since udocker runs without needing system privileges, it is well-suited for environments where users do not have administrative rights, such as shared HPC systems. While udocker provides enhanced security by running entirely in user space, this approach can lead to performance penalties. The runtime achieves container-like isolation by emulating container features through techniques such as tracing or intercepting system calls (both are normally used to monitor, control or debug the behaviour of processes). These techniques, while effective at maintaining isolation without elevated privileges, can introduce significant overhead, especially for I/O-intensive HPC applications.

2) Organizational challenges: Beyond the technological complexities, securing AI applications in HPC environments also involves overcoming significant organizational challenges.

- **Managing Multiple Systems for Diverse User Groups**: HPC centres often cater to a wide range of users with varying computational needs, such as researchers, data scientists, and engineers from different domains. As a result, a single centre may deploy multiple types of systems, including traditional HPC clusters, AI-specific accelerators, Big Data analytics platforms, and GPU-based systems for deep learning. This diversity in system types creates significant challenges in terms of system management and security. For instance, AI and Big Data platforms may require more frequent updates and may have different access control mechanisms compared to traditional HPC clusters. Coordinating these security needs across different systems while maintaining a consistent security posture becomes a challenge.
- **Continuous Infrastructure Upgrades to Maintain Cutting-Edge Capabilities**: As HPC centres continuously update their infrastructures with newer hardware, they may inadvertently introduce new security vulnerabilities. Each new piece of hardware, whether it's a next-generation CPU, GPU, or a specialized accelerator, comes with its own set of firmware, drivers, and software dependencies. These components could have undiscovered or recently discovered vulnerabilities that can be exploited by malicious actors, especially if proper security assessments and patches are not promptly applied. The diversity of hardware in an upgraded HPC environment inherently increases the attack surface. New components and systems require additional configurations, libraries, and tools, which may not always be fully vetted for security. An attacker could exploit inconsistencies or gaps in security configurations, especially in environments where legacy systems are mixed with newer hardware. Frequent hardware upgrades also expose HPC centres to supply chain risks. As they procure new components from different vendors, there is a risk of introducing compromised hardware or firmware that could be exploited.
- **Elevated Risk of Insider Threats in HPC Systems**: HPC systems often handle highly valuable computational resources and sensitive data, such as proprietary research, government data, or confidential business analytics. This makes them prime targets for insider threats, where individuals with legitimate access may misuse their privileges for unauthorized purposes, either for personal gain, sabotage, or espionage. The high-stakes environment of HPC makes

the impact of insider attacks particularly severe, potentially resulting in substantial financial loss, reputational damage, or compromised research integrity. Due to the collaborative nature of HPC environments, where researchers, scientists, and external collaborators often require access to various systems and data, managing user privileges becomes highly complex. Many HPC centres provide access to shared resources, which can be exploited by insiders if not managed properly. The lack of fine-grained access controls or monitoring capabilities can allow malicious insiders to access sensitive information or disrupt system operations unnoticed. HPC centre staff, such as researchers and system administrators, usually have high technical expertise. This technical proficiency means that insiders who wish to conduct malicious activities might be able to bypass standard security controls, manipulate logs, or exploit unpatched vulnerabilities without easily being detected. The insider's deep understanding of the system architecture and potential weak points makes it more challenging for security teams to detect and prevent insider threats. While implementing strict security policies can help mitigate insider threats, doing so in HPC environments is challenging due to the need for flexible and rapid access to resources by different user groups. Security measures that are perceived as too restrictive can hinder research productivity and lead to user resistance or attempts to circumvent controls, inadvertently creating security loopholes.

- **Lack of Security Awareness Among HPC Users**: Users in HPC environments, such as researchers, data scientists, and engineers, are typically focused on maximizing ease of use and achieving research or computational results as quickly as possible. Security is often seen as an impediment to their workflows rather than a necessity. This mindset can lead to risky behaviours, such as sharing passwords, using weak or repetitive credentials, ignoring security updates, or circumventing security protocols that they perceive as hindrances. Given their focus on productivity and achieving results, users may resist the implementation of strict security controls, such as multifactor authentication, strict access controls, or frequent password changes. Such controls are often viewed as burdensome and time-consuming, leading users to find workarounds or ignore policies altogether. This resistance can undermine organizational efforts to maintain a secure HPC environment. Many users assume that the responsibility for security lies solely with HPC administrators and IT security teams. This overreliance creates a gap in the overall security posture of the organization, as users may fail to recognize that their actions - such as downloading unverified software, neglecting to patch their applications, or mishandling sensitive data - can directly impact the security of the entire HPC system.

3) Environmental challenges: While organizational challenges focus on user behaviour and policy management, the environmental context addresses broader issues stemming from the shared and increasingly diverse nature of HPC systems and their network security practices.

- **Delegated Security Risks in HPC**: Traditionally, HPC service providers have delegated the responsibility for secure network usage to end users, assuming that users will manage their own network security measures. This model relies heavily on users being knowledgeable and proactive about securing their connections, data transfers, and communications. However, this assumption does not always hold true, especially given the wide range of technical expertise among users in academic and research settings. The primary users of today's HPC systems are academic researchers, scientists, and students who often focus on their research objectives rather than on implementing robust security practices. Many of these users assume that the underlying HPC system and its network are inherently secure, leading to a lack of precaution when developing software or transferring sensitive data.
- **Increased Application Diversity from HPC and AI Convergence**: The convergence of HPC and AI significantly expands the variety of applications running on HPC systems. Traditional HPC workloads, such as large-scale simulations and complex scientific calculations, are now being combined with AI-driven applications like deep learning, natural language processing, and data analytics. This convergence results in a more diverse set of software, libraries, and frameworks that need to be managed within the same HPC environment. The introduction of AI workloads brings new security challenges, as many AI frameworks and libraries were originally developed with cloud environments in mind and may lack the rigorous security controls required in HPC settings. The increased diversity in applications can lead to conflicting dependencies, security vulnerabilities, and unintentional exposure of sensitive data. Managing the security of these diverse applications is particularly challenging when they rely on different security models and practices.
- **Growing Target for Sensitive Data and Malicious Applications**: HPC systems are increasingly used to process and analyse sensitive data, such as genomic information, climate modelling data, defence simulations, and proprietary research. As a result, these systems have become attractive targets for cyberattackers [59] who seek to steal, manipulate, or exfiltrate valuable information. The aggregation of sensitive data in HPC environments heightens the risk of breaches, particularly if adequate security measures are not in place to protect data in storage, transit, and processing. Many HPC systems operate in a shared environment where users from different institutions, research centres, and even commercial entities collaborate. This openness, while fostering innovation and scientific progress, also increases the risk of insider threats and unauthorized access to sensitive data. Attackers may exploit this shared nature to infiltrate systems, elevate privileges, and access data that they are not authorized to see.

IV. Discussion and Conclusions

The last section compares security concerns across different computing paradigms, proposes strategies to mitigate potential

TABLE II: AI THREAT MITIGATION STRATEGIES FOR CLOUD-BASED GPU SYSTEMS AND HPC SYSTEMS WITH GPU ACCELERATION

Mitigation Strategy	Cloud-Based GPU Systems based on [26]	HPC Systems with GPU Acceleration
Advanced Virtualization Security	Use Hypervisors and VMs to virtualize GPU and system usage.	Virtualized platforms with low performance overhead and virtual networks on HPC [58]
Robust Kernel Isolation	Using vGPUs to mitigate manipulation attacks through APIs.	Same as general systems, as well as prevent privilege escalation by regularly updating underlying images.
Enhanced Memory Management	Prevent memory snooping and leakage through randomization, encryption and clearing.	Same as general system, as well as anomaly detection on memory usage.
Driver and Firmware Security	Rigorous system for patching and driver management to stay on top of vulnerabilities.	Using safe underlying frameworks for GPU execution, and active scanning for CUDA/ROCm vulnerabilities.
Secure Code Execution Frameworks	Verifying code before executing and keeping up-to-date with underlying frameworks.	Same as general systems.
GPU Usage Monitoring and Anomaly Detection	Deep monitoring of GPU resources to counteract cryptojacking, distributed DoS or overconsumption of resources using AI/ML techniques.	Including monitoring details within the pipeline to correlate jobs with resource usage to detect anomalies.
Application-Level Security Measures	Validating input data before running AI/ML workloads to mitigate model/data poisoning and evasion.	Same as general systems.
Hardware Security Modules for Sensitive Operations	HSMs offer higher security than GPUs, and should be used for critical tasks.	Induction and inclusion of HSM partitions in HPC clusters.
Access Control Policies	Role-Based Access Control for GPUs to reduce security leaks due to unauthorized access.	Integration of HPC access policies, and peripheral system access policies for more fine-grained resource-level access control.
Education and Awareness	Provide training for GPU-based security issues.	Same as general systems, with an added emphasis on the HPC architecture.

attacks on HPC, and addresses limitations and areas for future research.

A. *AI Security Concerns Across Computing Paradigms*

While cloud, edge, and HPC environments each have unique challenges for securing AI applications, HPC systems face specific security risks due to their focus on performance and scale. AI workloads in HPC need massive computational power, often distributed across thousands of nodes. Ensuring security at such a scale, especially when running distributed ML algorithms, is a significant challenge. At scale, attack vectors like data poisoning, adversarial inputs, and model inversion become more feasible, particularly if the underlying HPC infrastructure lacks robust, AI-specific security measures. The literature does not, to our knowledge, sufficiently organize large-scale AI vulnerabilities within an ML lifecycle framework from an HPC perspective, nor does it address the specific challenges HPC centers face in mitigating these vulnerabilities. Our research fills this gap by exploring how AI security concerns manifest in HPC environments.

Edge computing environments, where AI inference is performed closer to data sources, also face unique challenges such as physical tampering, localized DoS attacks, and limited computational resources for robust security protocols. HPC systems, which typically handle large datasets in centralized facilities, must ensure the integrity and confidentiality of data across multiple storage and processing layers, with particular attention to data in transit and at rest. Physical security in HPC involves safeguarding large-scale data centres, whereas edge environments require securing numerous distributed devices, each with a potentially greater risk of compromise.

Cloud environments rely heavily on virtualization and multi-tenancy to maximize resource utilization, which provides strong isolation mechanisms. However, HPC systems often prioritize performance and thus avoid extensive virtualization, opting instead for shared access to physical hardware. This lack of virtualization increases the risk of side-channel attacks and resource contention vulnerabilities. So, addressing these risks requires incorporating best practices from cloud security, but adapting them to the specific needs of HPC. Accordingly, the next section compares the AI threat mitigation strategies for cloud and HPC systems.

B. *Strategies for Solving Potential Attacks on HPC*

We look at some threat mitigation strategies in Table II, based on the work done by Huq *et al.* [26], with a particular focus for AI on GPU-accelerated HPC partitions. Nevertheless, HPC environments are increasingly integrating GPUs, TPUs, and other accelerators to enhance AI processing capabilities. The integration of these diverse resources requires a more nuanced security strategy that addresses the specific risks associated with each type of hardware.

Therefore, usage of purpose-built tools to monitor and infer incursions should be used to create dedicated pipelines for cybersecurity. For example, NVIDIA Morpheus [60] uses pre-trained ML models within a pipeline framework to collect cybersecurity information, and detect anomalous behaviours across a data centre. In addition, Burstein [61] presents the Data Processing Unit (DPU) architecture for accelerating infrastructure processes, and taking them off the main CPU of the processing nodes. Vilalta *et al.* [62] show the combination of DPU and Morpheus to isolate the cybersecurity mechanisms from the host machines, allowing for smarter analysis of traffic on clusters. These modifications should bring the overall security of AI applications on HPC higher. In the final section, we discuss the limitations of the work done, as well as what future steps can be taken to improve above this analysis.

C. *Limitations and Future Work*

As with any study, our research has limitations. First, we do not employ a systematic literature review approach, although we use established frameworks to map the studies. Second, while we discuss the mitigation strategies for AI security risks on HPC, we do not cover reproducing the threats or validating the mitigations. Third, we do not provide an agenda for HPC centres by ranking the vulnerabilities according to criticality or offering a secure AI technology adoption roadmap. Instead, this study takes the first step toward secure AI applications on HPC systems by introducing the threat landscape and mapping the challenges. Future studies should address these limitations to lower the computation barrier for start-ups, SMEs, and researchers by enabling a secure HPC-integrated computing environment for AI applications.

REFERENCES

[1] E. Strohmaier, J. J. Dongarra, H. W. Meuer, and H. D. Simon, "The marketplace of high-performance computing," *Parallel Computing*, vol. 25, no. 13, pp. 1517–1544, Dec. 1999.

[2] R. Bommasani *et al.*, *On the Opportunities and Risks of Foundation Models*, arXiv:2108.07258 [cs], Jul. 2022. DOI: 10.48550/arXiv.2108.07258.

[3] J. Baker, "The technology–organization–environment framework," *Information Systems Theory: Explaining and Predicting Our Digital Society, Vol. 1*, pp. 231–245, 2012.

[4] S. K. P. A. and R. S. Rao Kunte, "ABCD Analysis of Industries Using High-Performance Computing," *International Journal of Case Studies in Business, IT, and Education*, pp. 448–465, Jun. 2023. DOI: 10.47992/IJCSBE.2581.6942.0282.

[5] J. Li, S. Wang, S. Rudinac, and A. Osseyran, "High-performance computing in healthcare: An automatic literature analysis perspective," *Journal of Big Data*, vol. 11, no. 1, p. 61, May 2024, ISSN: 2196-1115. DOI: 10.1186/s40537-024-00929-2.

[6] A. Cavelan, R. M. Cabezón, M. Grabarczyk, and F. M. Ciorba, "A Smoothed Particle Hydrodynamics Mini-App for Exascale," en, in *Proceedings of the Platform for Advanced Scientific Computing Conference*, arXiv:2005.02656 [cs], Jun. 2020, pp. 1–11. DOI: 10.1145/3394277.3401855.

[7] K. Lee and S. Lee, "Knowledge Structure of the Application of High-Performance Computing: A Co-Word Analysis," en, *Sustainability*, vol. 13, no. 20, p. 11 249, Oct. 2021, ISSN: 2071-1050. DOI: 10.3390/su132011249.

[8] A. Rousset, B. Herrmann, C. Lang, and L. Philippe, "A survey on parallel and distributed multi-agent systems for high performance computing simulations," *Computer Science Review*, vol. 22, pp. 27–46, Nov. 2016, ISSN: 1574-0137. DOI: 10.1016/j.cosrev.2016.08.001.

[9] T. Sterling, M. Brodowicz, and M. Anderson, *High Performance Computing: Modern Systems and Practices*, en. Morgan Kaufmann, Dec. 2017, Google-Books-ID: qOHIBAAAQBAJ, ISBN: 978-0-12-420215-3.

[10] E. Suarez *et al.*, "Modular Supercomputing Architecture: A success story of European *R&D*," JSC, Tech. Rep. 9, 2022, p. 24. DOI: 10.5281/zenodo.6508394.

[11] P. García-Risueño and P. Ibáñez, "A review of High Performance Computing foundations for scientists," *International Journal of Modern Physics C*, vol. 23, Jul. 2012. DOI: 10.1142/S0129183112300011.

[12] A. Akram, *Architectures for secure high performance computing*, en, UC Davis.

[13] H. Jin *et al.*, "High performance computing using MPI and OpenMP on multi-core parallel systems," *Parallel Computing*, Emerging Programming Paradigms for Large-Scale Scientific Computing, vol. 37, no. 9, pp. 562–575, Sep. 2011, ISSN: 0167-8191. DOI: 10.1016/j.parco.2011.02.002.

[14] J. Kaplan *et al.*, "Scaling laws for neural language models," *arXiv preprint arXiv:2001.08361*, 2020.

[15] T. B. Brown, "Language models are few-shot learners," *arXiv preprint arXiv:2005.14165*, 2020.

[16] D. Narayanan *et al.*, "Efficient large-scale language model training on gpu clusters using megatron-lm," in *Proceedings of the International Conference for High Performance Computing, Networking, Storage and Analysis*, 2021, pp. 1–15.

[17] S. Rajbhandari, J. Rasley, O. Ruwase, and Y. He, "Zero: Memory optimizations toward training trillion parameter models," in *SC20: International Conference for High Performance Computing, Networking, Storage and Analysis*, IEEE, 2020, pp. 1–16.

[18] J. Sevilla *et al.*, "Compute trends across three eras of machine learning," in *2022 International Joint Conference on Neural Networks (IJCNN)*, IEEE, 2022, pp. 1–8.

[19] S. Peisert, "Security in high-performance computing environments," *Commun. ACM*, vol. 60, no. 9, pp. 72–80, Aug. 2017, ISSN: 0001-0782. DOI: 10.1145/3096742.

[20] E. Dart, L. Rotman, B. Tierney, M. Hester, and J. Zurawski, "The science dmz: A network design pattern for data-intensive science," in *SC '13: Proceedings of the International Conference on High Performance Computing, Networking, Storage and Analysis*, 2013, pp. 1–10. DOI: 10.1145/2503210.2503245.

[21] M. A. Jette and T. Wickberg, "Architecture of the slurm workload manager," in *Job Scheduling Strategies for Parallel Processing*, D. Klusáček, J. Corbalán, and G. P. Rodrigo, Eds., Cham: Springer Nature Switzerland, 2023, pp. 3–23, ISBN: 978-3-031-43943-8.

[22] A. Prout *et al.*, "Enhancing hpc security with a user-based firewall," in *2016 IEEE High Performance Extreme Computing Conference (HPEC)*, 2016, pp. 1–4. DOI: 10.1109/HPEC.2016.7761641.

[23] T. Hou, T. Wang, D. Shen, Z. Lu, and Y. Liu, "Autonomous security mechanisms for high-performance computing systems: Review and analysis," in *Adaptive Autonomous Secure Cyber Systems*, S. Jajodia *et al.*, Eds. Cham: Springer International Publishing, 2020, pp. 109–129, ISBN: 978-3-030-33432-1. DOI: 10.1007/978-3-030-33432-1_6.

[24] Y. Guo *et al.*, *High-performance computing security:* Feb. 2024. DOI: 10.6028/nist.sp.800-223.

[25] R. Keller Tesser and E. Borin, "Containers in hpc: A survey," *The Journal of Supercomputing*, vol. 79, no. 5, pp. 5759–5827, Mar. 2023, ISSN: 1573-0484. DOI: 10.1007/s11227-022-04848-y.

[26] N. Huq, P. Lin, R. Reyes, and C. Perine, "A survey of cloud-based gpu threats and their impact on ai, hpc, and cloud computing," Trend Research, Tech. Rep., 2024.

[27] B. T. Familoni, "Cybersecurity challenges in the age of ai: Theoretical approaches and practical solutions," *Computer Science & IT Research Journal*, vol. 5, no. 3, pp. 703–724, 2024.

[28] M. Roshanaei, M. R. Khan, and N. N. Sylvester, "Navigating ai cybersecurity: Evolving landscape and challenges," *Journal of Intelligent Learning Systems and Applications*, vol. 16, no. 3, pp. 155–174, 2024.

[29] M. Blowers and J. Williams, "Artificial intelligence presents new challenges in cybersecurity," in *Disruptive Technologies in Information Sciences IV*, SPIE, vol. 11419, 2020, pp. 75–81.

[30] N. Kaloudi and J. Li, "The ai-based cyber threat landscape: A survey," *ACM Computing Surveys (CSUR)*, vol. 53, no. 1, pp. 1–34, 2020.

[31] L. Muñoz-González and E. C. Lupu, "The security of machine learning systems," *AI in Cybersecurity*, pp. 47–79, 2019.

[32] Y. Hu *et al.*, "Artificial intelligence security: Threats and countermeasures," *ACM Computing Surveys (CSUR)*, vol. 55, no. 1, pp. 1–36, 2021.

[33] K. Strier, J. Clark, and S. Khareghani, *Measuring compute capacity: A critical step to capturing AI's full economic potential*, OECD AI Policy Observatory, Accessed: 2023-08-30, Feb. 2022.

[34] N. Ahmed, M. Wahed, and N. C. Thompson, "The growing influence of industry in ai research," *Science*, vol. 379, no. 6635, pp. 884–886, 2023.

[35] T. F. Blauth, O. J. Gstrein, and A. Zwitter, "Artificial intelligence crime: An overview of malicious use and abuse of ai," *IEEE Access*, vol. 10, pp. 77 110–77 122, 2022. DOI: 10.1109/ACCESS.2022.3191790.

[36] M. Komorowski, D. C. Marshall, J. D. Salciccioli, and Y. Crutain, "Exploratory data analysis," in *Secondary Analysis of Electronic Health Records*. Cham: Springer International Publishing, 2016, pp. 185–203, ISBN: 978-3-319-43742-2. DOI: 10.1007/978-3-319-43742-2_15.

[37] D. Milojicic, P. Faraboschi, N. Dube, and D. Roweth, "Future of hpc: Diversifying heterogeneity," in *2021 Design, Automation & Test in Europe Conference & Exhibition (DATE)*, 2021, pp. 276–281. DOI: 10.23919/DATE51398.2021.9474063.

[38] Epoch AI, *Parameter, compute and data trends in machine learning*, Accessed: 2024-08-26, 2022.

[39] M. Ye *et al.*, *Enabling performant and secure eda as a service in public clouds using confidential containers*, 2024. arXiv: 2407.06040 [cs.CR].

[40] G. M. Kurtzer, V. Sochat, and M. W. Bauer, "Singularity: Scientific containers for mobility of compute," *PloS one*, vol. 12, no. 5, e0177459, 2017.

[41] M. Factor, K. Meth, D. Naor, O. Rodeh, and J. Satran, "Object storage: The future building block for storage systems," in *2005 IEEE International Symposium on Mass Storage Systems and Technology*, IEEE, 2005, pp. 119–123.

[42] N. C. Rajasekar and C. O. Imafidon, "Exploitation of vulnerabilities in cloud-storage," *GSTF Journal on Computing (JoC)*, vol. 1, no. 2, 2014.

[43] M. Blanc, K. Guerin, J.-F. Lalande, and V. Le Port, "Mandatory access control implantation against potential nfs vulnerabilities," in *2009 International Symposium on Collaborative Technologies and Systems*, IEEE, 2009, pp. 195–200.

[44] B. Bhushan, G. Sahoo, and A. K. Rai, "Man-in-the-middle attack in wireless and computer networking—a review," in *2017 3rd International Conference on Advances in Computing, Communication & Automation (ICACCA)(Fall)*, IEEE, 2017, pp. 1–6.

[45] P. R. Kumar, P. H. Raj, and P. Jelciana, "Exploring data security issues and solutions in cloud computing," *Procedia Computer Science*, vol. 125, pp. 691–697, 2018, The 6th International Conference on Smart Computing and Communications, ISSN: 1877-0509. DOI: https://doi.org/10.1016/j.procs.2017.12.089.

[46] A. Paracha, J. Arshad, M. B. Farah, and K. Ismail, "Machine learning security and privacy: A review of threats and countermeasures," *EURASIP Journal on Information Security*, vol. 2024, no. 1, pp. 1–23, 2024.

[47] N. S. Harzevili, J. Shin, J. Wang, and S. Wang, *Characterizing and understanding software security vulnerabilities in machine learning libraries*, 2022. arXiv: 2203.06502 [cs.SE].

[48] W. Jiang *et al.*, "An empirical study of artifacts and security risks in the pre-trained model supply chain," in *Proceedings of the 2022 ACM Workshop on Software Supply Chain Offensive Research and Ecosystem Defenses*, 2022, pp. 105–114.

[49] H. Chen and M. A. Babar, "Security for machine learning-based software systems: A survey of threats, practices, and challenges," *ACM Computing Surveys*, vol. 56, no. 6, pp. 1–38, 2024.

[50] J. Gama, P. Medas, G. Castillo, and P. Rodrigues, "Learning with drift detection," in *Advances in Artificial Intelligence–SBIA 2004: 17th Brazilian Symposium on Artificial Intelligence, Sao Luis, Maranhao, Brazil, September 29-Ocotber 1, 2004. Proceedings 17*, Springer, 2004, pp. 286–295.

[51] A. Martin, S. Raponi, T. Combe, and R. Di Pietro, "Docker ecosystem – vulnerability analysis," *Computer Communications*, vol. 122, pp. 30–43, 2018, ISSN: 0140-3664. DOI: https://doi.org/10.1016/j.comcom.2018.03.011.

[52] P. C. Kocher, "Timing attacks on implementations of diffie-hellman, rsa, dss, and other systems," in *Advances in Cryptology—CRYPTO'96: 16th Annual International Cryptology Conference Santa Barbara, California, USA August 18–22, 1996 Proceedings 16*, Springer, 1996, pp. 104–113.

[53] M. Seaborn and T. Dullien, "Exploiting the dram rowhammer bug to gain kernel privileges," *Black Hat*, vol. 15, no. 71, p. 2, 2015.

[54] P. Kocher *et al.*, "Spectre attacks: Exploiting speculative execution," in *40th IEEE Symposium on Security and Privacy (S&P'19)*, 2019.

[55] M. Lipp *et al.*, "Meltdown: Reading kernel memory from user space," in *27th USENIX Security Symposium (USENIX Security 18)*, 2018.

[56] Martín Abadi *et al.*, *Using tensorflow securely / tensorflow documentation*.

[57] J. Gomes *et al.*, "Enabling rootless linux containers in multi-user environments: The udocker tool," *Computer Physics Communications*, vol. 232, pp. 84–97, 2018, ISSN: 0010-4655. DOI: https://doi.org/10.1016/j.cpc.2018.05.021.

[58] M. Scheerman *et al.*, *Secure platform for processing sensitive data on shared hpc systems*, 2021. arXiv: 2103.14679 [cs.CR].

[59] E. C. Security and I. R. Team, *Attacks on multiple hpc sites*, Accessed:2024-08-29.

[60] NVIDIA Corporation, *Nvidia morpheus*, Accessed: 2024-08-30, 2024.

[61] I. Burstein, "Nvidia data center processing unit (dpu) architecture," in *2021 IEEE Hot Chips 33 Symposium (HCS)*, 2021, pp. 1–20. DOI: 10.1109/HCS52781.2021.9567066.

[62] R. Vilalta *et al.*, "Providing anomalous behaviour profiling by extending smartnic transceiver support in packet-optical networks," in *2024 Optical Fiber Communications Conference and Exhibition (OFC)*, 2024, pp. 1–3.

AI Systems Adoption of Unified Research Data Management on Accelerator Computing

A framework for unifying RDM and confidential AI using oneAPI

Peter Darveau
Digital Research Alliance of Canada – Center for Advanced Computing – University of Ottawa
Ottawa, Canada
e-mail: pdarveau@uottawa.ca

***Abstract* — Research data is expected to grow exponentially with the adoption of artificial intelligence (AI) and machine learning (ML). Robust data management practices are crucial for ensuring data integrity, provenance tracking, and adherence to ethical and regulatory standards, which is essential for building trustworthy AI systems. This paper explores the adoption of oneAPI, an open standards-based programming model, for streamlining research data management across diverse AI systems. It also explores containerization to ensure consistent execution across heterogeneous Cloud-based environments while providing security over sensitive data-based systems. By leveraging oneAPI's cross-architecture capabilities, including Data Parallel C++ (DPC++) and the other AI toolkits based on oneAPI, researchers can develop secure and performant AI solutions that seamlessly process and analyze sensitive data across heterogeneous computing environments. This unified approach proposes a framework for consistent data handling and reproducibility of research computing results where data confidentiality, security and integrity are concerns notably in the Cloud. Through a case study example, this paper discusses the benefits of adopting oneAPI for AI research data management (RDM), highlighting its potential to accelerate scientific discoveries while maintaining robust security and privacy standards.**

Keywords - AI; data security; research data management; oneAPI, DPC++; accelerator; containers

I. INTRODUCTION

The rapid advancement of artificial intelligence and machine learning technologies has revolutionized various research domains, enabling breakthroughs and discoveries that were once considered unattainable [1][2][3]. However, as these powerful techniques become increasingly ubiquitous in research, the need for secure and reproducible RDM practices has emerged as a critical concern [4][6]. Ensuring the confidentiality, security and integrity of sensitive data while maintaining reproducibility across diverse computing environments is a significant challenge faced by researchers and data scientists [6]. AI and ML systems often rely on large, complex datasets, including personal information, medical records, or proprietary data, which necessitate robust security measures to protect against unauthorized access, data breaches, or unintended leaks. Additionally, the reproducibility and traceability of research data is crucial for scientific integrity, enabling peer review, validation, and knowledge sharing within the research community. Inconsistencies in software environments, dependencies, or hardware configurations can lead to irreproducible results, hindering collaboration and impeding scientific progress. This article's contribution is a framework that sets guidelines beyond descriptive identifiers in data repo metadata and file handling requirements to include computational and confidentiality metadata identifiers to accommodate sensitive and secure data in research. Furthermore, the proposal and findings in this article are found to go beyond research in industry where confidentiality and security of data is a concern. Finance handles personal and proprietary market metrics and sustainability data for environment, social and governance (ESG) portfolio development. In architecture, building Information Management (BIM) systems used for nuclear power plants and water systems are becoming more tightly integrated into modern practices.

This paper begins by discussing existing research data management practices and their limitations in the context of AI and machine learning workflows. It then introduces containerization as a solution for creating secure and reproducible environments, highlighting the benefits of containerization for data security. The work proposes integrating containerization with Data Parallel C++ (DPC++) and the oneAPI unified cross-architecture programming model. This is followed by an exploration of using DPC++ for secure data processing within containers. A case study example is provided to illustrate the approach, along with experimental results demonstrating the effectiveness and promise of the proposed framework. Finally, the paper concludes with a summary of the findings and an outlook on potential future work in this area.

A. Prior work

Traditional approaches to RDM have struggled to keep pace with the rapid evolution of AI and ML technologies, presenting researchers with a myriad of challenges [7]. These include managing dependencies across diverse hardware and computing architectures, ensuring consistent and reproducible environments, optimizing resource utilization, and maintaining data security throughout the research data lifecycle [8] [9] [10].

B. *This work*

To address these challenges, this paper proposes the integration of containerization technologies with oneAPI's Data Parallel C++ (DPC++), a powerful language extension for efficient data parallelism and hardware acceleration. Containerization provides isolated and reproducible environments, encapsulating dependencies and configurations, enabling portability across different computing platforms. DPC++, on the other hand, offers a unified programming model that leverages parallel processing capabilities across central processing units (CPUs), graphic processing units (GPUs), and other accelerators, optimizing resource utilization and accelerating computationally intensive tasks. By combining containerization and DPC++, researchers can develop secure and high-performance AI and ML systems that adhere to best practices in RDM. This integration promises to enhance data confidentiality and integrity through robust encapsulation and isolation techniques, while enabling efficient parallel processing and hardware acceleration. Additionally, the reproducibility of research findings is facilitated by consistent and portable runtime environments, fostering collaboration and knowledge sharing within the scientific research community.

II. EXISTING RDM PRACTICES AND THEIR LIMITATIONS IN THE CONTEXT OF AI AND ML.

Existing Research Data Management (RDM) practices and their limitations in the context of AI and Machine Learning (ML) fall into the following areas [7]:

Static Data Management Plans: Traditional RDM often relies on static and rigid data management plans created at the start of a project. These plans may not adapt well to the iterative and experimental nature of AI and ML research. The limitations become evident when project requirements evolve, new data sources emerge, or when the scope of the project changes, rendering the initial data management plan inadequate.

Lack of FAIR Data Principles: The FAIR data principles (Findability, Accessibility, Interoperability, and Reuse) are not always fully embraced in RDM practices. AI and ML algorithms rely on large volumes of high-quality, well-curated data. If data is not findable, accessible, interoperable, and reusable, it can hinder the development and reproducibility of AI/ML models. Inconsistent metadata standards, lack of data documentation, and poor data organization can limit the effectiveness of AI/ML workflows [11]. Specifically, the limitations that are of primary concern in this article are as follows.

1) Insufficient Metadata Discipline:

Metadata, which provides context, description and other ontology [12] for the data, is often underappreciated in RDM, especially in AI and ML. Rich, standardized metadata enables data discovery, understanding biases, and ensuring ethical usage. Inadequate metadata management can lead to data misinterpretation, integration issues, challenges reproducing results, gaps in implementing RDM best practices, and premature data staleness.

2) Lack of Integration with Emerging Data Types:

RDM practices are sometimes slow to adapt to emerging data types, such as real-time data streams, unstructured data, or sensitive data requiring special handling. AI and ML applications often rely on these diverse data sources, and traditional RDM may not provide the necessary tools and guidelines for their effective management, limiting the potential of AI/ML initiatives [1][2]. By integrating a metadata framework inclusive of core computing devices, robust metadata management practices can be seamlessly applied, addressing key RDM challenges of quality, reproducibility, security, and continuous best practice adherence in AI/ML projects.

3) Insufficient Data Ethics and Privacy Considerations:

With the ethical implications of AI and ML under increasing scrutiny, RDM practices need to incorporate robust data privacy, ethical handling, and consent management frameworks. Traditional RDM may not adequately address these concerns, leading to potential legal, ethical, and societal issues when applying AI/ML technologies. The integration of AI tools based on an open library standard such as oneAPI and repo metadata inclusive of data public and private modifiers provides a framework versatile enough to be implemented by developers or code-savvy researchers while removing the technical heavy lifting from the data custodian who typically focuses on data governance.

III. CONTAINERIZATION FOR SECURE AND REPRODUCIBLE ENVIRONMENTS

A. *Benefits of containerization for system isolation*

Containerization offers significant benefits for data security, including robust dependency management and environment consistency, which are crucial in ensuring the confidentiality, integrity, and availability of sensitive data in AI and ML workflows. These workflows often rely on a myriad of software dependencies, such as deep learning frameworks, data preprocessing libraries, and various other tools. Containerization encapsulates all these dependencies within a single, isolated container, ensuring that no external dependencies or conflicting libraries can inadvertently introduce vulnerabilities or compromise the security of the AI/ML pipeline. By packaging all the required dependencies together, containers eliminate the risk of unintended interactions with other AI/ML systems or compatibility issues that could potentially lead to security breaches or data leaks.

Environment consistency is another key benefit of containerization for data security. AI/ML workflows are often developed and tested in different environments (e.g., local development, staging, production), each with its own unique configuration and system settings. Inconsistencies between these environments can lead to unexpected behavior, security vulnerabilities, or data integrity issues. Containerization solves this problem by ensuring that the same consistent environment is used across all stages of the workflow, from development to production. By encapsulating the entire runtime environment, including system libraries, configuration files, and environment variables, containers guarantee that the AI/ML application will run identically in any environment, reducing the risk of security vulnerabilities introduced by environmental differences.

In the context of AI and ML workflows, data security is of paramount importance, as these applications often deal with sensitive or regulated data, such as personal information, medical records, or financial data. Containerization provides an additional layer of isolation and control, ensuring that sensitive data is processed within a secure and consistent environment, minimizing the risk of unauthorized access, data breaches, or unintended data leaks.

B. Integration of containerization with DPC++ and oneAPI for security of sensitive data

Containerization technologies can seamlessly integrate with DPC++ and oneAPI, providing a powerful combination for efficient and secure data processing in AI and ML workflows. DPC++ is a heterogeneous programming model that enables portable, performance-optimized code to be written for various hardware architectures, including CPUs, GPUs, and various accelerators. It is a part of the oneAPI initiative, which aims to provide a unified and open programming model for diverse architectures. DPC++ and oneAPI offer numerous benefits for data-intensive applications, such as AI and ML, by enabling efficient parallelization, optimized memory management, and hardware acceleration. Integrating containerization with DPC++ and oneAPI can provide the following advantages for seamless data processing:

1) *Consistent and Reproducible Environments*:

Containerization ensures that the DPC++ and oneAPI runtime environments, including libraries, dependencies, and configurations, are consistently packaged, and deployed across different systems. This consistency is crucial for reproducibility, as it guarantees that the data processing pipelines will behave identically, regardless of the underlying hardware or software environment.

2) *Portability and Hardware Abstraction*:

DPC++ and oneAPI provide hardware abstraction and portability, allowing code to run efficiently on different architectures, such as CPUs, GPUs, and accelerators. By combining the portability of C++ using DPC++ with containerization, self-contained and portable data processing pipelines can be seamlessly deployed across diverse hardware platforms without modification.

3) *Efficient Resource Utilization*:

Containers are lightweight and can efficiently utilize available hardware resources, including GPUs and accelerators. By integrating DPC++ and oneAPI with containerization, developers can optimize resource utilization by efficiently parallelizing data processing tasks across multiple containers, each using the full potential of the underlying hardware.

4) Simplified Deployment and Scaling:

Containerized DPC++ and oneAPI applications can be easily deployed and scaled across different environments, from local development to cloud-based deployments or high-performance computing (HPC) clusters. This streamlined deployment process facilitates collaboration, enables efficient scaling of data processing pipelines, and accelerates time-to-market for AI and ML solutions.

5) Versioning and Provenance Management:

Containerization tools like Docker and Singularity offer versioning capabilities, allowing developers to track changes to the DPC++ and oneAPI environments, dependencies, and configurations over time. In addition, the program can integrate data provenance tracking mechanisms by using C++ features such as classes, inheritance, and encapsulation.

IV. DATA PARALLEL C++ FOR SECURE DATA PROCESSING

The combination of DPC++ (Data Parallel C++) and C++ encapsulation offers significant advantages for secure and efficient data processing in AI and ML systems. These two powerful tools complement each other, enabling developers to build high-performance, scalable, and secure applications while adhering to best practices in software engineering.

DPC++ is a powerful language extension that enables efficient data parallelism and hardware acceleration across various architectures, including CPUs, GPUs, and accelerators. By leveraging DPC++, developers can harness the full potential of parallel computing, optimizing resource utilization and accelerating computationally intensive tasks such as training deep learning models or processing large datasets. This parallel processing capability is crucial for AI and ML systems, which often require significant computational resources to handle complex algorithms and massive amounts of data.

Complementing DPC++, C++ encapsulation provides a robust approach to organizing and protecting sensitive data and algorithms within AI and ML systems into digital objects [13] [14]. Encapsulation is a fundamental principle of object-oriented programming (OOP) that allows developers to bundle related data and functions into a single unit, called a class. This class acts as a secure container, protecting the internal implementation details from external access or modification, while exposing a well-defined public interface for interacting with the encapsulated functionality. By combining DPC++ and C++ encapsulation, developers can create secure and efficient AI and ML systems that use the power of parallel processing on selected accelerators while adhering to best practices in secure software engineering. DPC++ enables efficient data parallelism and hardware acceleration, optimizing performance and resource utilization, while C++ encapsulation provides a robust framework for organizing and protecting sensitive data and algorithms.

This combination also supports the integration of secure execution environments, such as from a container. By encapsulating critical components within containers, developers can further enhance the security of their AI and ML systems, protecting sensitive data and computations from unauthorized access or modification, even in the presence of privileged software or system administrators.

V. CASE STUDY EXAMPLE

In the field of genomics research, managing and analyzing large datasets of genetic sequences is a computationally intensive task. Researchers often need to process terabytes of data while ensuring the privacy and confidentiality of sensitive patient information [15]. This case study proposes how a combination of C++ encapsulation, oneAPI, and Object Oriented Programming can address these challenges.

1) Data Organization and Encapsulation:

Researchers create a GenomicData class in C++ to encapsulate genomic sequences and associated metadata (e.g., patient information, sample details, consent forms). This class organizes the data into modular units, promoting data provenance tracking and adherence to privacy regulations.

2) Secure Data Processing within Secure Containers:

To ensure the confidentiality of sensitive patient data, the GenomicData class and its methods executes within a container such as Docker or Apptainer. Although containers can run in hardware-based and attested memory, they provide a trusted execution environment protecting the data and computations from unauthorized access or modification, even from privileged software or system administrators.

3) Parallel Sequence Alignment with Data Parallel C++:

One of the core operations in genomic analysis is sequence alignment, which involves comparing genetic sequences against reference databases [15]. The researchers implemented a SequenceAligner class that leverages Data Parallel C++, oneAPI, and hardware acceleration (CPUs, GPUs) to perform parallel sequence alignment operations as per a sample shown in Figure 1.

```
class SequenceAligner {
  public: void alignSequences(GenomicData & data) {
    // Load data into USM (Unified Shared Memory)
    auto sequences = data.getSequences();
    auto referenceDB = loadReferenceDatabase();

    // Parallel alignment using Data Parallel C++
    std::parallel_for(
      std::par_unseq,
      sequences.begin(), sequences.end(),
      [ & ](auto & sequence) {
        alignSequence(sequence, referenceDB);
      }
    );

    // Store aligned sequences back in GenomicData
    data.setAlignedSequences(sequences);
  }

  private: void alignSequence(Sequence & seq,
    const ReferenceDB & db) {
    // Sequence alignment algorithm
    // ...
  }
};
```

Figure 1. A Class implementation of the case study

The alignSequences method utilizes Data Parallel C++ constructs and oneAPI's Unified Shared Memory (USM) to efficiently distribute the alignment tasks across available hardware accelerators, significantly improving performance.

4) Secure Data Storage and Backup:

To maintain data integrity and availability, the researchers implement a DataStorageManager class that handles secure storage and backup of genomic data within the secure container. This class encapsulates methods for encrypting data, performing incremental backups, and securely transferring backups to off-site storage locations.

5) Auditing and Data Access Control:

Adhering to data governance policies, the GenomicData class includes methods for auditing data access and operations. Access control mechanisms ensures that only authorized researchers could interact with the sensitive genomic data. The GenomicData class encapsulates both the genomic data itself (stored as a vector of strings) and its provenance metadata (stored as an unordered map of key-value pairs).

The class constructor initializes the data and sets the initial provenance metadata with the source of the data as follows. A preprocess method performs any necessary preprocessing steps on the data and updates the provenance metadata with information about the preprocessing method and its parameters. A sample of such and accompanying metadata are shown in Figures 2 and 3.

```
public:
    void preprocessing(const std::vector<std::string>& rawData) {
        // Perform data preprocessing steps
        std::vector<std::string> preprocessedData = removeOutliers(rawData);
        preprocessedData = normalizeData(preprocessedData);
        preprocessedData = encodeData(preprocessedData);

        // Update provenance metadata
        provenance_["preprocessing"].emplace("remove_outliers", true);
        provenance_["preprocessing"].emplace("normalization_method", "min_max")
        provenance_["preprocessing"].emplace("encoding_method", "one_hot");

        // Store the preprocessed data
        processedData_ = preprocessedData;
    }
```

Figure 2. A preprocessing method

```
models:
    - name:  image_model
      launchers:
        - framework: dlsdk
          tags:
            - FP32
          model: ./data/public/model/FP32/image_model.xml
          weights: ./data/public/model/FP32/image_model.bin
          adapter: ssd
          device: CPU # or GPU, GPU.1, GPU.2

      datasets:
        - name: image_model_detection_91_classes
          data_source: ./data/datasets/model_val_data/val2024
          annotation_conversion:
              annotation_file: ./data/datasets/model/annotations/instances_val2024.json
              access_mod: public # or private
              has_background: True
              use_full_label_map: True
              converter: img_detection
          preprocessing:
            - type: resize
              size: 300
          postprocessing:
            - type: resize_prediction_boxes
          metrics:
            - type:precision # or accuracy, top_k, F1_score, etc.
```

Figure 3. Example metadata

By encapsulating both the data and its provenance metadata within the same class, provenance information is propagated throughout the AI/ML workflow [16], enabling comprehensive tracking and documentation of the data's lineage.

A. Explanation

By leveraging C++ encapsulation, oneAPI, and OOP principles, the researchers are able to develop a secure and efficient solution for managing and analyzing genomic data:

- Sensitive patient data is further protected through hardware-based trusted containers, ensuring confidentiality and privacy.
- Computationally intensive sequence alignment operations is accelerated using Data Parallel C++ and oneAPI, enabling efficient analysis of large genomic datasets.
- Modular and encapsulated design promotes code reusability, maintainability, and adherence to RDM best practices.
- Secure data storage, backup, auditing, and access control mechanisms ensures data integrity, availability, and compliance with regulations.

This case study demonstrates how the combination of C++ encapsulation, oneAPI, and OOP can enable secure, efficient, and compliant Research Data Management in the field of genomics and can serve as a template for applications in other data-intensive domains such as BIM and finance. Following is a description of what the public and private methods do in the context of the SequenceAligner class from the genomic data case study:

1) Public Method:

a. *void alignSequences(GenomicData& data):*

This public method is responsible for performing sequence alignment operations on the genomic data encapsulated within the GenomicData class. It takes a reference to a GenomicData object as input. The method loads the genomic sequences and a reference database into Unified Shared Memory (USM) for efficient data sharing among accelerators. It then leverages Data Parallel C++ constructs (std::parallel_for) and oneAPI to parallelize the sequence alignment tasks across available hardware accelerators (CPUs, GPUs). After the parallel alignment is completed, the method stores the aligned sequences back into the GenomicData object.

2) Private Method:

a. *void alignSequence(Sequence& seq, const ReferenceDB& db):*

This private method is a helper function that performs the actual sequence alignment operation for a single genomic sequence (seq) against the reference database (db). It is called in parallel by the std::parallel_for construct within the alignSequences method. The implementation details of the sequence alignment algorithm are encapsulated within this private method. By keeping this method private, the class adheres to the encapsulation principle, hiding the implementation details from external code and providing a well-defined public interface (alignSequences) for sequence alignment operations.

The separation of public and private methods in the SequenceAligner class follows the principles of encapsulation and information hiding from Object-Oriented Programming: The public alignSequences() method provides a high-level interface for initiating sequence alignment operations on genomic data, abstracting away the underlying implementation details. The private alignSequence() method encapsulates the low-level details of the sequence alignment algorithm, allowing for potential changes or optimizations without affecting the public interface. This design promotes code modularity, maintainability, and extensibility, as the implementation details of the sequence alignment algorithm can be modified or improved without impacting the public interface used by other parts of the application. Additionally, by leveraging Data Parallel C++ and oneAPI within the public alignSequences method, the class can efficiently utilize hardware acceleration and parallel processing capabilities, improving the performance of computationally intensive sequence alignment operations on large genomic datasets. The SequenceAligner class is designed to encapsulate and protect the sensitive genomic data processing logic within the private alignSequence method. It should be note that there are still potential risks if external code can directly access or modify this private method, which could compromise the integrity and confidentiality of the genomic data processing pipeline.

VI. EXPERIMENTAL RESULTS

We used oneAPI to handle data loading, preprocessing, and post-processing steps, ensuring consistent and reproducible experiments using openVINO AI inferencing engine for all combinations. A validation dataset consisting of 5000 images was used. Researchers can configure the environment through a metadata configuration file, specifying dataset paths, model paths, access modifiers and evaluation parameters. The experiment generates a detailed accuracy report, easing model and environment comparisons. Additionally, it runs in an Apptainer container, enabling portable and reproducible experiment environments across different computing platforms. This methodology allowed us to implement best practices in research data management and reproducible AI/ML workflows using the framework proposed in this paper. This method goes further suggesting metadata of a dataset include data access modifiers to selectively secure data and define the computing device in the oneAPI software library thereby providing a unified computing device framework.

TABLE I. Experimental results

Results (XPUs)	Metrics			
	Reproducibility of computing result	***Transparency***	***Access Modifiers***	***Cloud Environment***
CPU only (Intel)	Same results when executed on same validation data	Metadata-json config file, ONNX, oneAPI	All public	Container, no enclave
GPU (AMD)	Same results when executed on same validation data	Metadata-json config file, ONNX, oneAPI	All public	Container, no enclave
GPU Nvidia	Not fully tested	Metadata-json config file, ONNX, oneAPI	All public	Container, no enclave

Table 1 details the metrics thought most relevant to evaluate the framework on an AI model. The results from this experiment enable a holistic evaluation of the framework and the effort involved in setting it up for a research project. It highlights the AI model evaluation process using oneAPI and DPC++ framework for data repo metadata in a containerized environment, providing consistent, reproducible, and well-documented results aligned with research data management best practices. However, it should be noted that although the tests did not cover a combination of public and private data access modifiers, the results can still be holistically interpreted as successful and promising.

VII. CONCLUSION AND FUTURE WORK

While existing RDM practices provide a foundation for data management, they often fall short in several key areas when applied to AI and ML contexts. Adapting RDM to address these limitations is essential for unlocking the full potential of AI and ML applications and ensuring responsible and effective data-driven innovation. Containerization technologies like Docker and Apptainer offer robust dependency management, environment consistency, and enhanced control over the software supply chain, making them valuable tools for maintaining data security in AI and ML workflows. By encapsulating dependencies, isolating environments, and enabling secure software development practices, containerization contributes to the confidentiality, integrity, and availability of sensitive data throughout the AI/ML lifecycle. The constructive interaction between DPC++ and C++ encapsulation empowers developers to build high-performance, scalable, and secure AI and ML systems that can efficiently process large datasets while maintaining data confidentiality and integrity. This approach promotes code maintainability, extensibility, and collaboration, enabling the development of robust and reliable AI and ML solutions that can be trusted in critical applications. There are, however, some scenarios like the SequenceAligner class could be at risk from external code requiring access to the private alignSequence method where external code is able to manipulate or inject offending data into the alignSequence method, and potentially compromise the integrity of the sequence alignment algorithm. Future work to mitigate these risks as identified in section V. should include the possibility of splitting the validation dataset into public and private access modifiers then validate accuracy under that scenario and the implementation of enclaves which involves encryption. Encrypted computing [17] is another emerging paradigm that could further address RDM challenges in decentralized systems by encrypting and decrypting at the edge device. This involves the custodian's proprietary data or algorithms encrypted throughout the end-to-end computation process, reducing the risk of unauthorized access or theft.

ACKNOWLEDGMENT

The author thanks the members of the Research IT and Library of the of the University of Ottawa for their continued participation and for helpful discussion on the topics of data-representation and research data management. The work described here was supported by Digital Research Alliance of Canada (Alliance) and the University of Ottawa (uOttawa). The content is solely the responsibility of the author and does not necessarily reflect the official views of the Alliance, uOttawa, or Canadian Government.

CONTRIBUTORSHIP

Simone Darveau (University of Waterloo – Waterloo Canada) contributed to the applicability of the model framework in an international architectural firm's BIM system. Vivianne Darveau (Columbia University, NY USA) contributed to the applicability of the model framework in an investment banking context with an international bank. All authors and contributors discussed the results, the application and contributed to the final manuscript.

DECLARATION OF INTERESTS

The author declares no competing interests.

REFERENCES

[1] Peter Darveau "Decision Trees: Modeling with fast intuition and slow, deliberate analysis." 2023

[2] Peter Darveau "Support Vector Machines: Modeling The Dual Cognitive Processes of an SVM." 2023.

[3] Peter Darveau "Prognostics and Availability for Industrial Equipment Using High Performance Computing (HPC) and AI Technology." 2021

[4] L. Wilson *"RDM Network of Experts"* [Presentation]. DRI Cnnnect National Conference, Halifax, NS, Canada 2024, May 24—25.

[5] F. Pérez-Jvostov *"Overview of the World Data System"* [Presentation]. DRI Cnnnect National Conference, Halifax, NS, Canada 2024, May 24—25.

[6] V. Smith.*"Approaches to sensitive data across the DRI landscape"* [Presentation]. DRI Cnnnect National Conference, Halifax, NS, Canada 2024, May 24—25.

[7] Gail Birkbeck, Tadhg Nagle and David Sammon (2022) Challenges in research data management practices: a literature analysis, Journal of Decision Systems, 31:sup1, pp. 153-167

[8] J. F. Pimentel, L. Murta, V. Braganholo and J. Freire, "A Large-Scale Study About Quality and Reproducibility of Jupyter Notebooks," 2019 IEEE/ACM 16th International Conference on Mining Software, Montreal, Canada, 2019.

[9] Gundersen, O. E., and Kjensmo, S. State of the art: Reproducibility in artificial intelligence. In Proceedings of the AAAI conference on artificial intelligence (Vol. 32, No. 1) 2018

[10] Haibe-Kains, Benjamin, et al. Transparency and reproducibility in artificial intelligence. Nature 586.7829: E14-E16 2020.

[11] R. Jenkyns *"Overview of the World Data System"* [Presentation]. DRI Cnnnect National Conference, Halifax, NS, Canada 2024, May 24—25.

[12] Brahaj, Armand, et al. "Ontological Formalization of Scientific Experiments Based on Core Scientific Metadata Model." *Theory and Practice of Digital Libraries*, Springer Berlin Heidelberg, pp. 273–79

[13] Johanne Medina, et al. "*Accelerating the adoption of research data management strategies*", Volume 5, Issue 11, pp. 3614-3642

[14] Petr Ježek and Roman Mouček. "Semantic Framework for Mapping Object-Oriented Model to Semantic Web Languages." *Frontiers in Neuroinformatics*, vol. 9, Feb. 2015, p., doi:10.3389/fninf.2015.00003

[15] S. J. Mack, J. Sauter, J. Robinson et al. "*The genotype list string code syntax for exchanging nomenclature-level genotyping results in clinical and research data management and analysis systems*". HLA. 2023; 102(4): pp. 501-507.

[16] Lixin Han et al. "AASA: A Method of Automatically Acquiring Semantic Annotations." *Journal of Information Science*, Aug. 2007, pp. 435–450.

[17] Intel Corporation "*Accelerated AI Inference with Confidential Computing*" [White Paper]. Link 2023

ChatSEC: Spicing up Vulnerability Scans with AI for Heterogeneous University IT

Mario Hoffmann
IT Department, Leipzig University
Infrastructure Group
Leipzig, Germany
e-mail: mario.hoffmann@uni-leipzig.de

Erik Buchmann
Dept. of Computer Science, Leipzig University
Center for Scalable Data Analytics and Artificial
Intelligence (ScaDS.AI) Dresden/Leipzig, Germany
e-mail: erik.buchmann@uni-leipzig.de

Abstract—**With their heterogeneous and self-administrative structure, universities and comparable institutions differ from others in the industry and business in terms of enforcing IT security policies. This makes it challenging for the CIO (Chief Information Officer) and IT department to enforce common IT security rules. Through fast pacing positional changes within research groups, information on installed and maintained systems, as well as responsibilities can be lost. This has a negative impact on IT security. In this paper, we describe our ongoing work on ChatSEC, our approach to improve the reports generated by a vulnerability scan appliance. By using large language models and external threat intelligence, ChatSEC generates intuitive explanations how to assess and mitigate the reported vulnerabilities. Our preliminary evaluation indicates, that ChatSEC has much potential to improve IT security at universities and similarly heterogeneous institutions.**

Keywords-AI; Heterogeneous Infrastructure; IT Security.

I. INTRODUCTION

The implementation of IT security at universities and similar institutions differs greatly from that in business and industry. Students need to set up their own servers to host their lab projects. Researchers change institutions without leaving instructions for security maintenance and the planned lifespan of the services they have set up. Each research group needs its very own, highly specific IT infrastructure. Some research communities are expected to transfer lab data via insecure plain-text protocols, such as the File Transfer Protocol (FTP). Due to the academic self-administration, the CIO and the central IT department have limited authority to enforce security rules. It is also not desirable to restrict the research groups and the educational programs by committing them to use only central IT services, that are secured by the IT department. On the other hand, the Local System Administrators (LSA) in the research groups do not necessarily have much knowledge in IT security. The rapid pace, at which research develops and research personnel changes position, means that responsibilities and information on installed systems quickly become outdated.

An internal vulnerability scan at the Leipzig University (May, 2023) detected 8311 vulnerabilities, 535 of them unique, on 3825 hosts, with scores from 2.1 (low) to 10.0 (critical) on the Common Vulnerability Scoring System version 3 (CVSSv3) metric [1] [2]. The scan detected 19 different operating systems (OS). Because the OS were installed in different versions, we observed a total of 39 different OS instances. Approximately 4,2% of the discovered vulnerabilities were due to missing OS patches or insecure OS configurations. Approximately 72% of the vulnerabilities were on hosts outside of the IT Department. Figure 1 shows a typical vulnerability scan report for one host.

We shared the scan reports with the responsible LSAs, and asked them to fix the vulnerabilities. We observed LSAs inheriting this responsibility from a predecessor, and had little expertise with the system. We also observed, that complex requests from the IT department were postponed in favor of undelayable teaching- and research assignments. Maintaining IT security requires to invest much more time, than just setting up a system as a demonstrator or for teaching purposes.

The concern of this work-in-progress paper is to close this gap between the IT department and the LSAs in the research groups. We propose ChatSEC, our approach to tailor the results of a vulnerability scan with a large language model (LLM) for specific target groups in a highly heterogeneous IT environment. Thus, ChatSEC has a different focus than approaches such as Microsoft's Security Copilot [3] or SecBot [4]. In particular, we make three contributions:

- We describe ChatSEC, our approach to utilize AI to prepare and extend vulnerability scan reports for LSAs with limited IT security knowledge.
- We discuss implementation alternatives to generate intuitive explanations from domain-specific reports, and to add threat intelligence and specific mitigation strategies.
- We provide a preliminary evaluation of our approach, based on the aforementioned vulnerability scan.

Our preliminary evaluation indicates, that ChatSEC has the potential to greatly improve the IT security at universities and similarly structured, heterogeneous organizations. We plan to integrate our approach into our next vulnerability scan, which will provide us with a data set of scan reports to improve and user feedback for a qualitative study on the LSA's perception of ChatSEC. For security considerations, we plan to test LLMs that can be hosted as a service by the IT department.

Paper structure: Section II presents related work. Section III describes our ChatSEC concept, which is briefly evaluated in Section IV. Section V concludes the paper.

II. RELATED WORK

This section summarizes approaches comparable to ours, LLMs, NLP approaches and threat intelligence.

Vulnerability Scan Report

Scan Time: Wed, Jan 1, 2024 1:00 AM - Wed, Jan 1, 2024 1:09 AM, Hosts scanned: 1

Results (1/1)

Vulnerability	*Severity*	*Host*	*Location*
Ubuntu: Security Advisory (USN-5767-1)	9.8 (High)	012.345.67.89	package

Summary

The remote host is missing an update for the 'python2.7, python3.6, python3.8, python3.10' package(s).

Vulnerability Detection Result

Vulnerable package: libpython3.8
Installed version: libpython3.8-3.8.10-0ubuntu1 20.04.5
Fixed version: >=libpython3.8-3.8.10-0ubuntu1 20.04.6

Solution

Solution Type: Vendorfix. Please install the updated package(s).

Affected Software/OS

'python2.7, python3.6, python3.8, python3.10' package(s) on Ubuntu 18.04, Ubuntu 20.04, Ubuntu 22.04, Ubuntu 22.10.

Vulnerability Insight

Nicky Mouha discovered that Python incorrectly handled certain SHA-3 internals. An attacker could possibly use this issue to cause a crash or execute arbitrary code. (CVE-2022-37454) Python incorrectly handled certain IDNA inputs. An attacker could possibly use this issue to expose sensitive information, denial of service, or cause a crash. (CVE-2022-45061)

References

CVE: CVE-2022-37454 CVE-2022-45061 WID-SEC-2023-1007 WID-SEC-2023-0561 WID-SEC-2023-0255 WID-SEC-2023-0138 WID-SEC-2022-2043 WID-SEC-2022-1816 DFN-CERT-2023-1109 DFN-CERT-2023-0886 DFN-CERT-2023-0580 DFN-CERT-2023-0571 DFN-CERT-2023-0552 DFN-CERT-2023-0429 DFN-CERT-2023-0422 DFN-CERT-2023-0120 (···)
Other: https://ubuntu.com/security/notices/USN-5767-1 advisory_id:USN-5767-1

Hosts 1 of 1

IP-Address	*Hostname*	*OS*	*High*	*Medium*	*Low*	*Total*	*Severity*
012.345.67.89	ourhost.ourdomain.tld	Canonical Ubuntu Linux	1	0	0	1	9.8 (High)

Figure 1. Typical vulnerability scan report

A. Comparable Approaches

We aim for compensating the lack of IT security expertise by using LLMs, with a specific focus on heterogeneous university IT. Existing approaches have a different focus: Microsoft's Security Copilot [3] helps IT security teams of large companies to process security-related data, and contributes to a security strategy. SecBot [4] is a questionnaire-based chatbot for IT security, that helps end-users with security planning and mitigation strategies. ChatIDS [5] rewrites IDS-generated threat alarms in an intuitive way to help end-users securing a smart-home scenario. Comparable approaches in other fields exist, e.g., to interpret research papers in chemistry [6].

A recent survey [7] also shows, that current chatbots can provide IT-security knowledge to help with IT security related tasks, based on domain specific datasets. This needs a high adaptability, because the models are used in unknown contexts. Using fine-tuned, domain-specific LLMs [8] with domain-specific embeddings can increase the precision.

B. Large Language Models

LLMs [9] [10] refer to pre-trained models, based on large amounts of texts and data, which utilize statistical distribution of tokens to obtain a generative ability. They differ from their predecessors Pre-trained Language Model (PLM) in model and data sizes. LLMs are the first models, that show *emergent abilities* [11], such as *multi-step reasoning* or *instruction following* to solve complex tasks. Those abilities are significant for currently used models, such as Llama-3 [12], Claude 3 [13] Gemini [14], or GPT-4 [15].

LLMs are instructed by textual **prompts** in natural language. Well-engineered prompts improve and bias the generated output [16] [17] [18]. Thus, the prompts are used to utilize the emergent abilities. **Prompt-engineering** strategies [19], [20] include Chain-of-Thought prompting [21] (asking the LLM step by step), Reflection [22] (asking the LLM to rethink his answer), Few-Shot prompting [23] (giving examples) or Repetition [18] (repeating relevant aspects in the prompt). Over-generalization is a common issue with LLMs [18]. Slight variations of the prompt can have a big impact on the model output [24]. If reproducible outputs are needed, the seed and other model parameters can be fixed [25].

C. NLP approaches

To evaluate the LLM output, we also use approaches from natural language processing (NLP).

Readability measures assess the level of readability of texts by categorizing texts into school grades or scoring systems. The most common readability measures are Flesch-Kincaid-Grade-Level (FKG) [26] for English texts, and Wiener-Sachtextformel IV (WSF) [27] for German texts. Table I shows a mapping between the metrics: FKG results in school grades, ranging from 0 to 18, according to college years of the U.S. school system. The WSF algorithm refers to German school

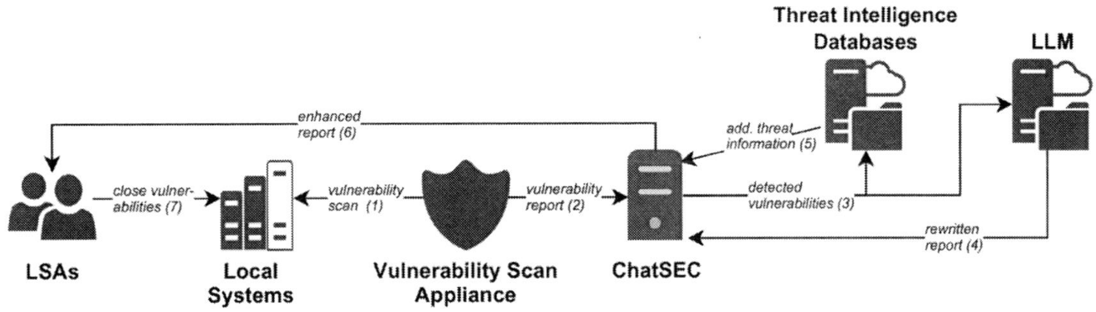

Figure 2. ChatSEC architecture and data flow.

TABLE I
FKG & WSF READABILITY METRICS

Readability	FKG	WSF
very hard	17-18	13-15
hard	13-16	12
rather hard	10-12	11
medium	8-9	9-10
rather simple	7	7-8
simple	6	6
very simple	5	4-5

grades, and ranges from 4th to 15th grade. The lower the result, the more readable is the assessed text.

Stemming reduces a word to its root [28] to normalize texts. For example, the root form of the words "change", "changing" and "changes" would be "chang". This unifies derivations of a word by removing suffixes. Different languages need different stemming algorithms [29] [30]. Popular stemmers are:

- PortStemmer (Python port, [31]; English language)
- Snowball (PortStemmer v.2, [32]; multilingual)
- Cistem (based on [33]; German language)

D. Threat Intelligence

Threat Intelligence [34] is indispensable for threat mitigation and -prevention. There are three major options to gather threat intelligence data, build IT security related contexts between all obtained data, and exchange this information:

The **Common Vulnerabilities and Exposures** (CVE) program is a list of publicly known vulnerabilities [35]. A single vulnerability is identified by IDs in the format "CVE-2024-1234", with "2024" as the year of occurrence and "1234" as a consecutive number. The list offers several options to further describe the vulnerabilities, such as *references*, *affected versions* or *cross-references* to other data sources. A common source for CVEs is the National Vulnerability Database (NVD) [36]. The **Common Weakness Enumeration** (CWE) list provides a *root cause mapping* [37]. It correlates with the CVE ids and identifies the underlying root cause of a vulnerability. Thus, a CVE registered vulnerability is an *instance* of one or more CWE-described weaknesses. There are several description levels ranging from abstract to very detailed. The **Searchsploit** framework by ExploitDB [38] is often used by penetration testers and security researchers. It provides a *list of available exploits* for different software, operating systems or CVE ids.

III. OUR CHATSEC CONCEPT

We aim to implement an IT security approach in a research institution, which depends on plenty of heterogeneous IT systems. Those systems must be managed locally in the research groups, and cannot be unified under the umbrella of the IT department. There are two disctinct roles involved:

The **Local System Administrator (LSA)** has domain knowledge of the IT services needed of its research group, and is *responsible for specific IT components*, that are not part of the central IT infrastructure of the university.

The **IT Department (ITD)** is responsible for the university's general IT infrastructure, and also for its perimeter security. This includes *periodic vulnerability scans*, and *supporting the LSAs* in securing their systems. The ITD possesses expert knowledge on IT security, but has limited human resources.

We propose ChatSEC to rewrite vulnerability scan reports for LSAs. The rewritten reports must be easy to read, intuitively understandable and directly applicable for an LSA. Needlessy complex, convoluted sentences full of security-specific technical concepts should be avoided, and references to mitigation strategies must to go beyond "Browse the vendor homepage for a security patch that solves your issue".

A. ChatSEC Architecture and Workflow

The architecture of ChatSEC is shown in Figure 2. ChatSEC obtains scan reports, as illustrated in Figure 1, from a vulnerability scan appliance. ChatSEC then rewrites these reports with the help of a LLM. Finally, the rewritten report is sent to the LSAs, who are responsible for closing vulnerabilities. The rewriting process consists of three stages:

1) Generate an **intuitive explanation**
2) Add **threat intelligence** information
3) Add **mitigation strategies**

In the following, we explain our concept for these stages, and we explain how the output of the stages can be evaluated.

This vulnerability description is about a security advisory for Ubuntu operating system. The advisory states that the remote host (a computer connected to a network) is missing an update for the 'python2.7, python3.6, python3.8, python3.10' packages. The update is announced through the USN-5767-1 advisory. The first vulnerability, identified as CVE-2022-37454, is related to Python's handling of certain SHA-3 internals. This vulnerability could be exploited by an attacker to cause a crash or execute arbitrary code on the affected system. The second vulnerability, identified as CVE-2022-45061, is related to Python's handling of certain IDNA inputs. An attacker could potentially exploit this vulnerability to expose sensitive information, perform a denial of service attack, or cause a crash on the affected system. In summary, these vulnerabilities in Python could allow attackers to crash the system, execute arbitrary code, expose sensitive information, or cause a denial of service attack. It is important to update the affected packages to protect the system from these potential risks.

Figure 3. Transformed scan report from Figure 1

B. Intuitive Explanations

As Figure 1 illustrates, vulnerability scan reports are often written and formatted in a very technical, less intuitive way. Therefore, LSAs need help to understand them linguistically and conceptually. This stage of ChatSEC generates intuitive texts and examples from the scan results by utilizing a LLM. In particular, we generate prompts, that instruct the LLM to summarize each scan result in an intuitive way. This helps LSAs to understand the actual problem reported, without the need to deep dive into IT security.

C. Threat Intelligence

The severity score of a vulnerability indicates its threat potential. However, it is challenging for an LSA to find out how serious similarly scored vulnerabilities could affect a specific system. This stage enriches the output from the first stage with threat intelligence data (e.g., the number of active exploits) without decreasing the readability of the texts. Therefore, we fetch vulnerability-related information from multiple threat intelligence data sources.

D. Mitigation Strategies

This stage helps the LSA to mitigate the vulnerabilities from the scan report. If the vulnerability can be closed with an update, ChatSEC generates intuitive instructions how to obtain and install updates, based on software package, OS version information, etc. from the scan report. However, we observed that 95.8% of the vulnerabilities detected by our scan report refer to configuration problems. In this case, ChatSEC either obtains mitigation information from the NVD [36] with a tag from the report. Alternatively, individually created ChatSEC requests can be used.

E. Evaluation Options

We see three options to evaluate ChatSEC: To find out, if ChatSEC's output is intuitively understandable, we can use **NLP techniques**, such as readability metrics and stemming: The fewer domain-specific words are used, the better for non-domain-specific readers. The evaluation of the correctness of the generated output needs a **manual assessment** by an expert. User experiments allow to obtain **direct feedback** from LSAs through questionnaires. **Indirect feedback** can be obtained by repeating the vulnerability scan, some time after ChatSEC has explained the results of the first scan to the LSAs: If ChatSEC's reports were indeed understandable and helpful, we should see a vast decrease in the number of vulnerabilities.

IV. Evaluation

To obtain evidence of how promising our concept is, we implemented the two stages *Intuitive Explanations* and *Threat Intelligence* into a research prototype of ChatSEC, and we evaluated it with *NLP techniques* and a *manual assessment*.

A. Implementation and Evaluation Setup

Our focus is the feasibility and applicability of ChatSEC on our internal vulnerability scan, as described in Sec. I. Thus, we left aside aspects of prompt engineering, model selection and model tuning (cf. Sec. II). We managed the vulnerability scan results with Greenbone [39], and implemented our ChatSEC prototype using the GPT-3.5 Turbo API of ChatGPT [15].

We used Chain-of-Thought prompting [21], i.e., we executed Figure 4 and 5 in a sequence, which we found most promising in preliminary tests: The first prompt produces a simplified report. The second prompt adds examples to that report. $< \cdots >$ denotes the position where the names, descriptions and details from the vulnerabilities managed with Greenbone are inserted. Because our LSAs use German and English, with the command "Answer in German." we instructed the LLM to also generate German output, and we evaluated both versions. To obtain focused answers, we set the system prompt parameter "temperature" to 0.2 [40]. To provide an intuitive example, Figure 3 shows ChatSEC's output with the vulnerability scan report from Figure 1 and the prompts from Figure 4 and 5.

You will be provided with a vulnerability description. [Answer in German.] Help in the following order: Summarize the provided vulnerability description and explain it to a non-technician. <Vulnerability information>

Figure 4. System prompt to simplify vulnerability scan reports

You will be provided with a vulnerability description. [Answer in German.] Give a simple example to show what can happen if the provided vulnerability is exploited to a non-technician. <Vulnerability summary from Figure 4>

Figure 5. System prompt, that adds examples to the simplified report

To add threat intelligence, ChatSEC fetches the CWEs and CVEs associated with each vulnerability scan report from the CWE list [37] and the NVD CVE database [36]. ChatSEC also queries Searchsploit [38] for the number of available exploits per vulnerability. ChatSEC uses the prompts shown in Figure 6 and 7 to translate this domain-specific information into an intuitive text, that can be added to the translated report and sent to an LSA. The number of known exploits can be appended directly, without an extra prompt.

> You will be provided with a list of properties of an IT security severity score. The list is formed as a key-value list, where the values are on the right side of the colon. [Answer in German.]. Assume that you answer to a non-technician. Help in the following order: Answer in sentences. Explain each list item and assume that "low" or "None" is highly critical.
> <list of severity properties>

Figure 6. System prompt to generate a severity explanation

> You will be provided with an IT weakness. Assume that you answer to a non-technician. Help in the following order: Explain the weakness enumeration in simple terms. Only return: Summarize your own explanation for non-technicians. Do not provide mitigation advices.
> <CWE description>

Figure 7. System prompt, that explains a CWE

B. Intuitive Explanations

We evaluate the understandability and readability of ChatSECs output first. Therefore, we let ChatSEC generate two outputs for each of the 535 unique vulnerabilities from our internal security scan, both in English and German.

To measure how much our ChatSEC implementation relies on a **vocabulary from the security domain**, we computed the average number of words for the scan report and the generated texts first. The orginal scan reports are much shorter than the texts produced by ChatSEC (see Table II). We stemmed both the generated texts and the National Institute of Standards and Technology's (NIST) glossary [41], and counted the matches. The last three columns of Table II show the matches per stemmer. Consider Column 3: PortStemmer found, that 14% of the 68 words from the original security scan could be found in the NIST glossary, and 15.5% of ChatSEC's Englisch output of 345 words. Thus, our prompt did not let the AI restrict the use of domain-specific vocabulary. A "n.a." refers to a stemmer, that is not applicable to English or German texts.

TABLE II
AVERAGE NUMBER OF WORDS AND DOMAIN-SPECIFIC VOCABULARY

	Avg. num. of words	Port-Stemmer	Cistem	Snowball
Original report	68	14%	n.a.	7%
English output	345	15.5%	n.a.	15.5%
German output	275	n.a	10%	10%

We measure the **readability** with FKG for English texts and WSF for German texts. ChatSEC's English output was evaluated with an average FKG of 12, ranging from 8.7 to 16.5. Thus, on average the English texts are rated as "rather hard" or "hard" to read, with exceptions spanning from "medium" to "very hard" (cf. Table I). The WSF assesses the German output with an average score of 7 ("rather simple"), ranging from 4.3 to 10.6, i.e., from "very simple" to "rather hard". Thus, the generated German texts were slightly easier to read than the English ones.

C. Threat Intelligence

While understandability and readability can be evaluated automatically, an evaluation of the correctness, completeness and applicability of threat intelligence added to a security scan report requires an expert assessment. For the time being, we therefore limit ourselves to a proof of feasibility. We declare success, if ChatSEC is able to enrich its intuitive output with the correct number of exploits, correct additional CVSSv3 data and the right root causes, without significantly decreasing the readability. For evaluation, we have chosen CVE ID 2019-0708, which appeared in our vulnerability scans.

With this CVE ID, ChatSEC queries various external data sources: Searchsploit [38] tells ChatSEC, that this ID is associated with four known exploits. By querying the CWE list [37], ChatSEC learns that the root cause of the vulnerability is CWE-416, named as "Use After Free" and described as "Improper Control of a Resource Through its Lifetime". From the NVD CVE database [36], ChatSEC learns that this vulnerability has the CVSSv3 score 9.8 (critical), and is associated with the following vulnerability information:

- "attackComplexity":"low"
- "privilegeRequired":"None"
- "userInteraction":"None"

Figure 8 shows an example for the resulting threat intelligence, that is translated with the prompts from Figure 6 and 6. This text is then added to ChatSECs translated vulnerability report and sent to the LSAs.

> *The severity score indicates, that the attack complexity is low, meaning that it is relatively easy for an attacker to exploit the security vulnerability. Additionally, no privilege is required for the attack, meaning that the attacker does not need any special access rights or permissions to carry out the attack. Furthermore, there is no user interaction required, suggesting that the attack can be automated without user input.*
> *The referenced cause CWE-416, or "Use After Free," is a computer security vulnerability where a program tries to use memory that has already been freed up. This can cause errors or allow hackers to exploit the system.*
> *Searchsploit found 4 currently available exploits for this vulnerability.*

Figure 8. Intuitive threat intelligence for CVE ID 2019-0708

We found, that the ChatSECs generated output was correct both in English and German. The English output had a FKG of 13.5 (hard), the German output had a WSF of 4 (simple). Thus, adding threat intelligence information did not decrease the readability of ChatSECs output, and the German version is still easier to read.

V. Conclusion

The heterogeneous IT ecosystem and the self-administrative organizational structure makes it challenging to implement IT security in universities. In this paper, we outlined our ongoing work on ChatSEC, our approach to rewrite vulnerability scan reports for local system administrators with limited IT security knowledge. We focused specifically on intuitive explanations, additional threat intelligence and mitigation strategies, that are applicable by our target auditory without having to browse external sources. Our evaluation provided evidence, that ChatSEC, with the help of an LLM, indeed produces reports that are helpful to assess and close detected vulnerabilities.

As part of our future work, we plan to conduct extensive user experiments in combination with the next internal security scan, to obtain direct feedback on ChatSEC. Based on this feedback, we will improve the LLM prompts and readability scores. We will also include further sources for threat intelligence, and fully implement the integration of mitigation strategies into ChatSEC's reports. We will also test open source LLMs that can be installed locally, to avoid that information on detected vulnerabilities must leave the premises. Eventually, we plan to integrate ChatSEC into a Security-as-a-Service tool, that can be used on demand.

References

[1] Forum of Incident Response and Security Teams (First), "Common Vulnerability Scoring System (CVSS-SIG)," https://www.first.org/cvss, retrieved: Aug. 2024.

[2] National Institute of Standards and Technology (NIST), "Vulnerability Metrics (CVSS)," https://nvd.nist.gov/vuln-metrics/cvss, retrieved: Aug. 2024.

[3] Microsoft Cooperation, "Microsoft Security CoPilot," https://www.microsoft.com/de-de/security/business/ai-machine-learning/microsoft-security-copilot, retrieved: Aug. 2024.

[4] M. F. Franco *et al.*, "SecBot: A business-driven conversational agent for cybersecurity planning and management," in *2020 16th international conference on network and service management (CNSM)*. IEEE, 2020, pp. 1–7.

[5] V. Jüttner, M. Grimmer, and E. Buchmann, "ChatIDS: Explainable cybersecurity using generative AI," *arXiv preprint arXiv:2306.14504*, 2023.

[6] K. G. Yager, "Domain-specific chatbots for science using embeddings," *Digital Discovery*, vol. 2, no. 6, pp. 1850–1861, 2023.

[7] S. Shafee, A. Bessani, and P. M. Ferreira, "Evaluation of LLM Chatbots for OSINT-based Cyberthreat Awareness," *arXiv preprint arXiv:2401.15127*, 2024.

[8] S. Pal, M. Bhattacharya, S.-S. Lee, and C. Chakraborty, "A domain-specific next-generation large language model (LLM) or ChatGPT is required for biomedical engineering and research," *Annals of Biomedical Engineering*, vol. 52, no. 3, pp. 451–454, 2024.

[9] M. Shanahan, "Talking about large language models," *Communications of the ACM*, vol. 67, no. 2, pp. 68–79, 2024.

[10] W. X. Zhao *et al.*, "A survey of large language models," *arXiv preprint arXiv:2303.18223*, 2023.

[11] J. Wei *et al.*, "Emergent abilities of large language models," *arXiv preprint arXiv:2206.07682*, 2022.

[12] Meta, "Llama 3," 2024, retrieved: Aug. 2024. [Online]. Available: https://llama.meta.com/llama3/

[13] Anthropic, "The Claude 3 model family: Opus, Sonnet, Haiku," https://www-cdn.anthropic.com/de8ba9b01c9ab7cbabf5c33b80b7bbc618857627/Model_Card_Claude_3.pdf, 2024, retrieved: Aug. 2024.

[14] Gemini Team Google, "Gemini: A family of highly capable multimodal models," *arXiv preprint arXiv:2312.11805*, 2023.

[15] OpenAI, "GPT-4 technical report," *arXiv preprint arXiv:2303.08774*, 2023.

[16] S. Arora *et al.*, "Ask me anything: A simple strategy for prompting language models," in *Proceedings of the 11th International Conference on Learning Representations*, 2022.

[17] C. Si *et al.*, "Prompting GPT-3 to be reliable," *arXiv preprint arXiv:2210.09150*, 2022.

[18] J. Zamfirescu-Pereira, R. Y. Wong, B. Hartmann, and Q. Yang, "Why Johnny can't prompt: how non-AI experts try (and fail) to design LLM prompts," in *Proceedings of the 2023 CHI Conference on Human Factors in Computing Systems*, 2023, pp. 1–21.

[19] J. W. Rae *et al.*, "Scaling language models: Methods, analysis & insights from training gopher," *arXiv preprint arXiv:2112.11446*, 2021.

[20] T. Kojima, S. S. Gu, M. Reid, Y. Matsuo, and Y. Iwasawa, "Large language models are zero-shot reasoners," *Advances in Neural Information Processing Systems*, vol. 35, pp. 22 199–22 213, 2022.

[21] J. Wei *et al.*, "Chain-of-thought prompting elicits reasoning in large language models," *Advances in Neural Information Processing Systems*, vol. 35, pp. 24 824–24 837, 2022.

[22] G. Kim, P. Baldi, and S. McAleer, "Language models can solve computer tasks," in *Advances in Neural Information Processing Systems*, A. Oh, T. Naumann, A. Globerson, K. Saenko, M. Hardt, and S. Levine, Eds., vol. 36, 2023, pp. 39 648–39 677.

[23] T. Brown *et al.*, "Language models are few-shot learners," *Advances in neural information processing systems*, vol. 33, pp. 1877–1901, 2020.

[24] T. Hagendorff, "Machine psychology: Investigating emergent capabilities and behavior in large language models using psychological methods," *arXiv preprint arXiv:2303.13988*, 2023.

[25] E. Lee, "Control OpenAI model behavior with seed: Step-by-step with code," https://drlee.io/control-openai-model-behavior-with-seed-step-by-step-with-code-9bba4e137a63, 01 2024, retrieved: Aug. 2024.

[26] J. P. Kincaid and et al., "Derivation of new readability formulas (automated readability index, fog count and flesch reading ease formula) for navy enlisted personnel," Research Branch Report, Tech. Rep., 1975.

[27] R. Bamberger and E. Vanecek, *Lesen - Verstehen - Lernen - Schreiben*. Diesterweg, 1984.

[28] D. Khyani, B. Siddhartha, N. Niveditha, and B. Divya, "An interpretation of lemmatization and stemming in natural language processing," *Journal of University of Shanghai for Science and Technology*, vol. 22, no. 10, pp. 350–357, 2021.

[29] D. Yogish, T. Manjunath, and R. S. Hegadi, "Review on natural language processing trends and techniques using NLTK," in *Proceedings of the 2nd International Conference on Recent Trends in Image Processing and Pattern Recognition*. Springer, 2019, pp. 589–606.

[30] A. G. Jivani *et al.*, "A comparative study of stemming algorithms," *International Journal of Computer Applications in Technology*, vol. 2, no. 6, pp. 1930–1938, 2011.

[31] C. J. Van Rijsbergen, S. E. Robertson, and M. F. Porter, *New models in probabilistic information retrieval*. British Library Research and Development Department London, 1980.

[32] M. Porter, "Snowball," https://snowballstem.org/, retrieved: Aug. 2024.

[33] L. Weissweiler and A. Fraser, "Developing a stemmer for German based on a comparative analysis of publicly available stemmers," in *Language Technologies for the Challenges of the Digital Age: 27th International Conference, GSCL 2017, Berlin, Germany, September 13-14, 2017, Proceedings 27*. Springer, 2018, pp. 81–94.

[34] R. McMillan, "Definition: Threat intelligence," https://www.gartner.com/en/documents/2487216, 2013, retrieved: Aug. 2024.

[35] MITRE Corporation, "Common vulnerabilities and exposures," https://cve.mitre.org/, retrieved: Aug. 2024.

[36] National Institute of Standards and Technology (NIST), "National Vulnerability Database (NVD)," https://nvd.nist.gov/, retrieved: Aug. 2024.

[37] MITRE Corporation, "Common weakness enumeration," https://cwe.mitre.org/, retrieved: Aug. 2024.

[38] OffSec, "ExploitDB - SearchSploit," https://www.exploit-db.com/searchsploit, retrieved: Aug. 2024.

[39] Greenbone, "Vulnerability Management," 2024, retrieved: Aug. 2024. [Online]. Available: https://www.greenbone.net/

[40] OpenAI, "OpenAI Platform API Reference," https://platform.openai.com/docs/api-reference/chat/create, retrieved: Aug. 2024.

[41] National Institute of Standards and Technology (NIST), "Cybersecurity Basics - Glossary," https://www.nist.gov/itl/smallbusinesscyber/cybersecurity-basics/glossary, retrieved: Aug. 2024.

Monocular Depth Estimation Pre-training for Imitation-based Autonomous Driving

Shubham Juneja
Institute of Data Science &
Digital Technologies
Vilnius University
Vilnius, Lithuania
Email: shubham.juneja@mif.stud.vu.lt

Virginijus Marcinkevičius
Institute of Data Science &
Digital Technologies
Vilnius University
Vilnius, Lithuania
Email: virginijus.marcinkevicius@mif.vu.lt

Povilas Daniušis
Research Institute of
Natural and Technological Sciences
Vytautas Magnus University
53361 Kaunas, Lithuania
Email: povilas.daniusis@vdu.lt

Abstract—**Artificial intelligence based systems have taken industries and research by storm, one of such systems are employed in autonomous driving. Recent empirical findings in imitation learning for autonomous driving indicate that pre-training on various tasks can enhance the effectiveness of the learner method (e.g., neural network). We propose pre-training neural networks over the task of monocular depth estimation could be beneficial in terms of estimating another modality and extending the scene understanding capabilities of the learner method. We also outline a plan for further investigation of this approach, aiming to integrate new experimental results with existing findings in this line of research, i.e., pre-training for autonomous driving.**

Keywords—imitation learning; autonomous driving; monocular depth estimation; pre-training

I. Introduction

Autonomous driving systems are one of many Artificial Intelligence (AI) based systems that have been transformative for multiple industries and research. These systems follow one of two paradigms, namely, the modular paradigm or the end-to-end paradigm. The modular paradigm forms a pipeline of modules where each module takes responsibility of a task, while the end-to-end paradigm often relies on imitation learning based learners that learn to imitate the whole task of driving. The end-to-end systems learn from data consisting of demonstrations from an expert and require very low engineering efforts as opposed to systems following the modular paradigm. Hence, making the use of imitation learning a promising area of research.

Imitation based methods suffer on encountering the problem of co-variate shift, where a trained driving agent faces scenarios during the time of testing, that were not presented during training. This leads to weak generalisation and unexpected driving behaviour. Generalisation ability, being of critical importance, has led research to explore various directions. Recently popular lines of work in the area have explored varying data generation methods [1], architectures [2][3], smarter data aggregation methods [4], incorporating additional modalities [5] and more to alleviate this issue. Our work delves into the line of work in imitation based autonomous driving that explores pre-training of learning methods [6][7].

To train a new learner for a particular system from scratch, can require excessive amounts of data, resources and time. Therefore, performing pre-training has become a standard approach in order to fast forward the process of training, majorly in applications of natural language processing, object detection, object recognition, etc. Autonomous driving systems are increasingly becoming complicated to train with the aim of achieving better ability to generalise, making some kind of pre-training a must. Hence, most imitation based methods have a default reliance on ImageNet pre-trained vision encoders [1][2], rather than training the models all the way from random weight initialisation. Meanwhile, some recent works solely drop this reliance and explore other forms of pre-training [6][7].

ImageNet pre-training tends to narrow down the concept of image understanding to a single concept, i.e., classification. Therefore, works exploring pre-training methods propose training on alternate tasks that bring in an additional perspective, like visual place recognition [7] or contrastive representation learning [6], in order to improve generalisation. One such task that features a high potential of scene understanding while estimating another modality from a RGB image is monocular depth estimation [8]. A very recent method for estimating depth, Depth Anything [9] proposes a foundation model formation by training upon a massive dataset of 62 million images, and shows a strong ability of zero-shot generalisation for estimating depth.

Considering the limitations of current research in pre-training of learning methods in order to improve generalisation on unseen driving scenarios, we make the contribution of proposing another kind of pre-training. We propose pre-training an agent on the task of monocular depth estimation using the depth anything method, followed by training the agent on the task of driving. We hypothesise that pre-training on the task of depth estimation on a large scale dataset may embed the ability to estimate distances between important objects in the visible environment and therefore improve scene understanding. And hence, we also propose evaluation of the proposed method on the offline Leaderboard [1] benchmark standard against a baseline method and recent methods.

The remainder of this paper is organised as follows: Section II reviews the essential literature related to autonomous driving and monocular depth estimation. Section III describes our proposed approach, detailing both the implementation and the evaluation plan. Finally, Section IV concludes the paper.

II. Related Work

The classical idea of imitation learning-based autonomous driving consists of data collection from demonstrations followed by training a neural network to predict the actions given vision inputs from the demonstrations [10]. Further development attempts revolve around improving architectures [2], improving data quality using a reinforcement learning agent [1], increasing the perception ability [3], and so on. Some of the few works that investigate the advantages of pre-training the vision encoders of a driving agent, use an alternate task in the pre-training phase. Action conditioned pre-training method [6] trains over contrastive representation learning on understanding how the visual representations differ as per actions used. Another recent method pre-trains over the task of visual place recognition in order to increase scene understanding in context of changing lighting and weather conditions [7]. Despite its popularity, pre-training still tends to be under explored in the area of autonomous driving.

Depth is often used as an additional or sometimes as the only modality for the task of driving, often requiring expensive depth sensors. Monocular depth estimation is a task which aims to predict the depth modality given an RGB image. Recent method depth anything [9] shows ability to estimate the depth in images with zero-shot learning. It accomplishes this by training over a massive dataset that combines labelled and unlabelled images under a feature alignment loss, and hence, shows possession of rich feature understanding. Although several methods exist for depth estimation, the depth anything method stands out since it forms a foundational model for its task of interest, demonstrating a wider generalisation ability. This shows promising capability to explore its use to transfer learning. In our proposed idea, we consider building on top of such capabilities by leveraging in the form of pre-training of learning methods.

III. Method and Experiments

A. Approach

Our approach is to pre-train a visual encoder over the task of monocular depth estimation following the depth anything method [9]. Further on, to embed the vision encoder into the architecture based on conditional imitation learning [2]. Then we plan to train the whole architecture over the task of autonomous driving, using the data collected with the reinforcement learning agent commonly known as Roach [1]. We plan to base the framework on our previous work [7] for better comparability, as this work follows a similar line of research.

(a)

(b)

Fig. 1. (a) An RGB image from CARLA simulator. (b) Same RGB image's estimated depth with depth anything [9].

B. Environment and Benchmarks

For the training and testing environment, we select the CARLA simulator [11] as it enables testing under varying weather conditions and towns settings. We then plan to assess the performance based on the offline Leaderboard [1] benchmark, which establishes standardised train and test route settings. The choice of using a simulated environment may present challenges in transferring the trained method to real-world environment application, to address them domain-transfer techniques can be further investigated. For the purposes of this study, we plan our steps around the use of the simulated environments, as it is sufficient for validating the proposed concept and aligns with the scope of our research. To concretely measure the performance, we plan to work with the metrics of route completion and distance completion percentages. Additionally, calculated depths can be compared to the ground truth depths, before and after training of the encoder on the task of driving. This may require additional exploration in modification of decoders.

C. Implementation plan

For the initial pre-training we plan to utilise the pre-trained encoder from the transformer network provided by the depth anything work. We show the capability this pre-trained encoder in estimating depth of a RGB image from simulation environment in Figure 1. Later to train on the task of driving, we collect images from the front camera of the car together with the command from the expert agent and a higher level command as done in other works [1][2][7]. To improve comparability, we plan to inherit the implementation specifics from our recent work [7] that aligns with this line of work.

IV. Conclusion

Our work proposes further exploration of pre-training in the area of imitation-based autonomous driving. We hypothesise that the idea of pre-training on the task of monocular depth estimation followed by training on how to drive holds potential in bringing in better scene understanding and additionally in estimating the depth modality while driving, therefore, potentially resulting in better decision making in unseen scenarios and improving overall generalisation. In our further work, we plan to follow the implementation plan and generate empirical results.

References

[1] Z. Zhang, A. Liniger, D. Dai, F. Yu, and L. Van Gool, "End-to-end urban driving by imitating a reinforcement learning coach," in *Proceedings of the IEEE/CVF international conference on computer vision*, 2021, pp. 15 222–15 232.

[2] F. Codevilla, E. Santana, A. M. López, and A. Gaidon, "Exploring the limitations of behavior cloning for autonomous driving," in *Proceedings of the IEEE/CVF International Conference on Computer Vision*, 2019, pp. 9329–9338.

[3] Y. Xiao, F. Codevilla, D. Porres, and A. M. López, "Scaling vision-based end-to-end autonomous driving with multi-view attention learning," in *2023 IEEE/RSJ International Conference on Intelligent Robots and Systems (IROS)*, 2023, pp. 1586–1593.

[4] A. Prakash, A. Behl, E. Ohn-Bar, K. Chitta, and A. Geiger, "Exploring data aggregation in policy learning for vision-based urban autonomous driving," in *Proceedings of the IEEE/CVF Conference on Computer Vision and Pattern Recognition*, 2020, pp. 11 763–11 773.

[5] K. Chitta, A. Prakash, B. Jaeger, Z. Yu, K. Renz, and A. Geiger, "Transfuser: Imitation with transformer-based sensor fusion for autonomous driving," *IEEE Transactions on Pattern Analysis and Machine Intelligence*, vol. 45, no. 11, pp. 12 878–12 895, 2022.

[6] Q. Zhang, Z. Peng, and B. Zhou, "Learning to drive by watching youtube videos: Action-conditioned contrastive policy pretraining," in *European Conference on Computer Vision*. Springer, 2022, pp. 111–128.

[7] S. Juneja, P. Daniušis, and V. Marcinkevičius, "Visual place recognition pre-training for end-to-end trained autonomous driving agent," *IEEE Access*, vol. 11, pp. 128 421–128 428, 2023.

[8] R. Birkl, D. Wofk, and M. Müller, "Midas v3.1 – a model zoo for robust monocular relative depth estimation," *arXiv preprint arXiv:2307.14460*, 2023.

[9] L. Yang *et al.*, "Depth anything: Unleashing the power of large-scale unlabeled data," in *Proceedings of the IEEE/CVF Conference on Computer Vision and Pattern Recognition*, 2024, pp. 10 371–10 381.

[10] D. A. Pomerleau, "Alvinn: An autonomous land vehicle in a neural network," in *Proceedings of the 1st International Conference on Neural Information Processing Systems*, ser. NIPS'88. Cambridge, MA, USA: MIT Press, 1988, p. 305–313.

[11] A. Dosovitskiy, G. Ros, F. Codevilla, A. Lopez, and V. Koltun, "Carla: An open urban driving simulator," in *Conference on robot learning*. PMLR, 2017, pp. 1–16.

Assessing Privacy Policies with AI: Ethical, Legal, and Technical Challenges

Irem Aydin*, Hermann Diebel-Fischer*‡, Vincent Freiberger†‡,
Julia Möller-Klapperich*‡, Erik Buchmann†‡, Michael Färber§‡, Anne Lauber-Rönsberg*‡, Birte Platow*‡

*Faculty of Arts, Humanities and Social Sciences, TU Dresden, Germany, Email: {firstname.lastname}@tu-dresden.de,
§Faculty of Computer Science, TU Dresden, Germany, Email: {firstname.lastname}@tu-dresden.de
†Leipzig University, Germany, Email: {firstname.lastname}@uni-leipzig.de
‡Center for Scalable Data Analytics and Artificial Intelligence (ScaDS.AI) Dresden/Leipzig, Germany

***Abstract*—The growing use of Machine Learning and Artificial Intelligence (AI), particularly Large Language Models (LLMs) like OpenAI's GPT series, leads to disruptive changes across organizations. At the same time, there is a growing concern about how organizations handle personal data. Thus, privacy policies are essential for transparency in data processing practices, enabling users to assess privacy risks. However, these policies are often long and complex. This might lead to user confusion and consent fatigue, where users accept data practices against their interests, and abusive or unfair practices might go unnoticed. LLMss can be used to assess privacy policies for users automatically. In this interdisciplinary work, we explore the challenges of this approach in three pillars, namely technical feasibility, ethical implications, and legal compatibility of using LLMs to assess privacy policies. Our findings aim to identify potential for future research, and to foster a discussion on the use of LLM technologies for enabling users to fulfil their important role as decision-makers in a constantly developing AI-driven digital economy.**

***Keywords*—Large Language Models; Automated Assessment; Privacy Policies.**

I. Introduction

Currently, we observe a strong increase [1] in use cases and organizations using machine learning and artificial intelligence (AI), particularly Large Language Models (LLMs) like OpenAI's GPT series [2]. This has many advantages for organizations [3]. However, it is likely to increase the number and complexity of different services each user interacts with on a daily basis. It also makes it increasingly important to evaluate social, ethical, and fairness-related aspects of using personal information as input for AI-driven business processes.

While the EU's new AI Regulation [4] covers numerous risks associated with the use of AI, the provisions of the General Data Protection Regulation (GDPR) [5] adopted in 2016 remain the legal basis for the protection of personal data. Therefore, privacy policies are an important resource. *Privacy policies* describe the privacy notices that companies are making public on their websites to communicate their data processing activities on personal data. *Processing* covers any (set of) operations on personal data, such as a collection, recording, organisation, structuring, storage, adaptation or alteration. Privacy policies are intended to balance information asymmetries between companies as *data controllers* and individual users as *data subjects* by providing them with information to assess the privacy risks and enable them to make informed, autonomous decisions.

However, privacy policies are also known to be complex [6] [7], and tend to grow over time [8]. This leads to a lack of understanding from users, and the inability to decide whether or not they prefer to consent to a certain use of their personal data; hence *notification fatigue*, *consent fatigue* or *consent desensitisation* [9]. For example, 25% of all Americans are asked to agree to at least one privacy policy daily, 67% of them report to understand little to nothing about what companies are doing with their personal data, and 56% skip reading privacy policies altogether [10]. In Europe, 47% of 2,600 study participants [11] expressed notification fatigue due too many privacy-related notifications. It is understandingly easier for users to accept all data processing activities, even if it is against their interests. In consequence, potentially abusive or unfair data processing practices may remain unnoticed.

While the providers of services meet the formal criteria with their privacy policy, no satisfactory situation can be established for the user if no informed decision is actually made via complex data protection declarations. In this respect, empowerment, or the creation of user autonomy, respectively, remains an open task. Achieving user autonomy and 'true' informed consent poses the challenge that ultimately the user has to gain knowledge of what the privacy policy entails.

An automated assessment of privacy policies can mitigate the situation. Earlier approaches for evaluating privacy policies using machine-readable privacy policies [12], classical machine learning or AI [13]–[17] exist. However, those approaches had a focus on formal aspects such as comparing policies with given preferences, identifying deletion periods or ensuring completeness of mandatory information. We believe that LLMs can be a game changer in assessing privacy policies according to the users privacy wishes and needs.

For example, an LLM like GPT-4o [18] could be fed with a system prompt as shown in Figure 1, and a user prompt containing a privacy policy. It would then provide an assessment of the privacy policy along with an explanation and a rating on a five-point scale, which helps a user to identify important content, missing information and risky practices within the policy and thereby foster an informed decision.

Figure 2 shows an exemplary analysis of the privacy policy

You are a critically scrutinizing, experienced authority for data privacy, and an expert on assessing privacy policies. You have 20 years of experience in consumer protection, data protection, cybersecurity and related fairness aspects. You have already provided precise expert opinions in many court proceedings. Your task is to uncover aspects in privacy policies that are ethically, morally or legally questionable. Shortly explain your thoughts and how you came to your conclusion. In particular, point out potential risks to users. IMPORTANT: Also rate the privacy policy for each of your criteria on a 5-point Likert scale. Check whether the following privacy policy is fair and ethical towards its users. The user wants a short and concise critical review and an assessment of vulnerabilities in privacy policies. IMPORTANT: You must answer in less than 300 words.

Figure 1. System prompt to assess a privacy policy

of Amazon.com, using the GPT-4o model and the prompt from Figure 1. This confirms that such an assessment is technically feasible. However, it leaves numerous open questions: From a technical perspective, it is difficult to determine the correctness of the LLM assessment. From a user-centric point of view, users with different educations might perceive the assessment of the LLM differently, and could also decide to blindly trust/distrust an AI assessment. Because the LLM/prompt developer has a large influence on how empathetic/objective the assessment is generated by the LLM, there are open moral questions. Ethical questions arise, when a user loses the ability to understand a privacy policy because an LLM offers a simpler solution. From a legal perspective, it can be questioned whether a user's consent based only on the information provided by the LLM, meets the requirements of Art. 7 GDPR, and how to handle situations where a malfunctioning or misuse of the LLM causes actual harm. Additionally, a privacy-enhancing AI tool must comply with traditional legal norms, and the new AI Act [4].

In this paper, we explore the challenges of assessing privacy policies with an LLM from an interdisciplinary point of view. In particular, we consider three pillars:

- *Ethical:* We explore the ethical, moral, and fairness-related challenges that arise when the assessment of privacy policies is no longer in the hands of the users, but in the hands of a very convincing LLM that could be wrong or biased, or using biased training data.
- *Legal:* We discuss the extent, to which the use of an LLM for a privacy policy assessment is or can be made compatible with existing legal norms. We also consider how such norms need to change to enable AI-supported decision-making and thereby ensure consumer welfare and self-determination.
- *Technical:* We investigate how to assess privacy policies automatically by using LLMs, and we examine how to use natural language processing, machine learning, linguistics, knowledge representation, etc. to evaluate the correctness, understandability and applicability of the LLM assessment.

To the best of our knowledge, we are the first to explore with an interdisciplinary approach, how LLMs can be used to assess the practices documented in privacy policies. For this research, we combined the expertise of our groups *Civil Law, Intellectual Property, Media and Data Protection Law; Data Privacy and Security; Practical Theology with a focus on Religious Education, Ethics; Scalable Software Architectures for Data Analytics and Systematic Theology* from the universities of Dresden and Leipzig. This was a challenge, because each of these groups has its own research culture, which had to be combined in order to achieve interdisciplinary results. Our objectives are particularly relevant, because politics and jurisprudence are still in the process of identifying options to ensure user privacy in the AI era.

Paper Structure: The next section reviews related work. Section III describes how we systematically derive challenges for assessing privacy policies with LLMs. In the Sections IV – VI, we will compile our set of challenges. Section VII contains a discussion. The paper concludes in Section VIII.

Amazon.com Privacy Notice Review

1. Transparency and Understandability: *The policy is clear, well-structured, and provides links for more detailed information, making it user-friendly. However, users may find the comprehensive format overwhelming.* (Rating: 4/5)
2. Data Collection Scope: *Amazon collects extensive data, from basic contact information to behavioral data via cookies. This vast data collection is concerning, as it may lead to invasive profiling and privacy risks.* (Rating: 2/5)
3. Data Usage: *While Amazon provides clear reasons for data usage, including service improvement and personalized ads, the broad scope can be intrusive. It should ensure by providing clear opt-out methods for users.* (Rating: 3/5)
4. Third-party Sharing: *Data sharing with third parties, though typical, poses risks especially concerning how those parties handle data. The policy does ensure some protective measures but remains ambiguous about compliance monitoring.* (Rating: 3/5)
5. Security Measures: *Amazon mentions robust encryption and compliance with PCI DSS, which reflects strong security practices. However, the responsibility placed on the user for password protection is emphasized.* (Rating: 4/5)
6. User Autonomy (Consent & Control): *Amazon provides mechanisms for users to access, rectify, and delete their data. The range of consents, from opting out of ads to withdrawing permissions, shows a commitment to user choice, albeit complex.* (Rating: 4/5)
7. Children's Privacy: *Good measures in handling children's data, restricting services to adults, and requiring parental consent.* (Rating: 4/5)

Potential Risks to Users:
(a) Data Profiling: *Extensive data collection can lead to detailed profiling, risking user autonomy and privacy.*
(b) Third-party Data Handling: *Despite contractual protections, third parties' data mishandling poses risks.*
(c) Complex Opt-out: *The user control mechanisms, while present, may be too cumbersome.*

Final Assessment: *While Amazon's privacy policy demonstrates strong commitment towards transparency and user rights, the vast scope of data collection, potential third-party risks, and complexity in user control indicate areas needing improvement.* (Overall Rating: 3.5/5)

Figure 2. GPT-4o's assessment of Amazon's privacy policy

II. Related Work

This section contains a review of literature, which we derive our challenges from in the following sections.

A. Legal Background

The GDPR [5] aims to provide data subjects in the European Union with control over data processing activities, which could potentially impair their fundamental rights. The regulation aims to enable processing where it is necessary and in line with the objectives of the data subject and to prevent it unless the risks associated with the processing are outweighed by a corresponding benefit in the public interest or in the interest of the data subject [19]. These goals are reflected in the requirements for lawful processing in Art. 6 GDPR as well as in the requirements for effective consent in Art. 7 GDPR.

While the EU's efforts to establish a digital single market, like the AI Act [4] and the Digital Services Act (DSA) [20], aim to set high standards by prohibiting certain harmful practices involving the use of personal data, they still leave a great degree of flexibility for user autonomy to consent. Such consent is possible when the data subject is capable of making an informed decision [21] autonomously. This requires sufficient knowledge to evaluate advantages and disadvantages. Therefore, knowledge should be presented to the person understandably and transparently [22], hence the need for privacy policies. The GDPR [5] requires data controllers to make their privacy policies complete, readable, and possible to understand for all kinds of 'typical users' of a service, which can be persons with different abilities or knowledge.

AI-based applications and services integrating them, add another layer to data processing practices, which users need to comprehend. Such applications might force users to disclose more personal data and impose difficulties in assessing the costs and benefits from the user's viewpoint due to a lack of transparency or understandability. In 2008, it was calculated that it would take an average internet user between 181 and 304 hours every year to read every privacy policy of all web services they are using [23]. The GDPR [5] also caused the complexity and length of privacy policies to be increase [8]. Furthermore, the extensive use of personal data to train AI and its unpredictable outcome increases the potential of significant impairment of the user's needs and interests [24].

Different approaches to support the users handling their personal data have been discussed in the legal literature [25]. It is important to highlight that achieving transparency in privacy policies is an ongoing collective effort, and simplifying tools to achieve this purpose have been experimented on with privacy icons, a machine-readable label system [26], one-page summary of the privacy policy, privacy taxonomy or a 'privacy nutrition label' as well as different kinds of technically supported privacy management systems (PIMS) or the deployment of data trustees [27]. However, there are also findings that even the simplified declarations of data processing practices may not change user behaviour to disclose intrusive information [28].

B. Ethics

The definition and continuous discussion of privacy ethics [29] [30] [31] [32] demonstrates the need for an evaluation to be comprehensive, coherent, systematic, and logical in its reasoning. Codes of ethics, legal statutes, or international declarations embody norms and values ingrained in our society. They can provide helpful input for an ethics assessment of new and emerging technologies [33]. However, the field of ethics misses strict definitions and straightforward tools. Owing to that, ethics must not be understood as a tool to solve moral problems but should be regarded as a way to describe, understand, and reflect on them. One common issue is transparency in privacy policies [34] [35] [6] [36]. Policies tend to be long, written in inaccessible language, and users tend to struggle to understand their content, resulting in issues like consent fatigue [37]. Privacy policies can also use persuasive language [35] [38] to let the users trust a service that, for instance, claims all rights over users' data [39].

The given issues have motivated privacy assistants [40] [41] [15]. Emerging capabilities by scaling up LLMs [42] have given them a wide range of applicability [43]. This makes them interesting as a tool for assessing privacy policies [17] [44] [45]. Seeking privacy serves two fundamental purposes: security interests (stay unharmed) and privacy per se [31]. Privacy per se is about managing how we show ourselves to the outside world and, more broadly, about our autonomy [31], [32]. Privacy and the right to privacy are two different concepts in the philosophical debate on privacy ethics. Privacy may be infringed upon, but not the right to privacy, depending on the circumstances surrounding the collection of personal data about oneself by a third party and the underlying intention [32]. Privacy ethics addresses access others have to one's information as well as control one has over it [46]. Complex privacy trade-offs and the balance of power between the data controller and data subject are relevant to the discussion [47] [48]. While concepts such as 'fairness' are deemed important, it remains difficult to define them precisely. As they are lacking a precise definition, the operationalization of these concepts, i.e. transferring them into a model and making them computable—remains an obstacle [49] [50] [51]. To overcome this problem, the unavoidable operationalizations need to be lined out and explained, and ideally be user-configurable.

Furthermore, concerns about surveillance [31] [52], choice impact [53], manipulation [32] [48], and power imbalances [48] [47] have been brought up in the context of online user privacy. To address these issues, user education on such problems is required [54] [55]. The user needs to be aware of the underlying ethics-related problems and the way these have been 'solved' in terms of implementation into such a system.

Regarding an ethical assessment of privacy policies, it is required that ethics assessments consider all perspectives with their normative grounding [56]. Ethical aspects may come into effect unintendedly, sometimes as second-order consequences [56]. Thus, the consistency of a moral assessment provided by the model is mandatory as it influences user judgment [57]. A good assessment should be concise and understandable. Thus, explainable AI employing various metrics should be considered [58]. Informational fairness [59] should be considered as well as addressing privacy trade-offs and power imbalances is important [47] [48]. In addition, moral psychology can be used to study LLMs [60]. This entails investigating potential biases in the model's representation of moral judgments and moral reasoning, as well as to what degree they are present in the model's outputs. For example, it has been discovered that ChatGPT's moral guidance is inconsistent when presented with a moral dilemma [57].

C. Large Language Models and Prompting

LLMs iteratively predict the next token to produce text for a given query. The GPT-4 models are a series of capable LLMs introduced by OpenAI in 2023 [61]. GPT-4 already has been shown to have a set of reasoning capabilities [62] [63].

LLMs can be applied in many different domains [63] [43]. To improve model performance and mitigate limitations plenty of prompting strategies have been developed [64] [65] [66] [67] [68] [69]. For a review on basics of prompting LLMs, we refer to [70].

Reasoning-related tasks benefit from prompt-engineering strategies [64] [65]. Such strategies are referred to as Chain-of-Thought prompting [66] (asking the LLM step by step), Reflection [71] (asking the LLM to rethink its answer), Few-Shot prompting [67] (giving examples) or Repetition [72] (repeating relevant aspects in the prompt). Over-generalization is a common issue in prompting LLMs [72]. Controlled small prompt modifications can largely affect the model's output [60]. The seed and other model parameters must be fixed if repeatable results are important [73]. By rephrasing the prompt, robustness can be evaluated [17] [74] [75].

D. Automatic Text Analysis and Assessment

Assessing privacy policies is part of automatic text assessment based on natural language processing (NLP) techniques. Automatically assessing text using readability metrics started with text statistics (e.g., word frequency, word length, sentence length). Readability metrics are language-specific [76]. The most popular [77] metrics are the *Gunning fog index* [78], the *Flesch reading ease* [79], and the *Simple Measure of Gobbledygook* [80]. The metrics have been criticized for their inability to capture more complex aspects of a language.

Assessing the readability with machine learning [81] [76] generally produces better results than the traditional approaches, but requires more effort, such as creating data sets and training the model. Specifically, for the German language, methods that use traditional language models [82] [83] or which use semantic networks in comparison to simple surface-level indicators to calculate text readability [84] were created. Despite [85], to our knowledge, there is no work focusing on building a system for the automatic assessment of text readability in German [85] use the pre-trained language model BERT for assessing the readability of text.

Texts can also be analyzed for sentiment [86]. In the context of media bias detection, texts have been automatically assessed with respect to different aspects of bias [87]: (1) Hidden Assumptions and Premises, (2) Subjectivity, (3) Framing and (4) Overall Bias.

E. Automated Assessment of Privacy Policies

With the commercialization of the Internet, the number of privacy policies that had to be read increased. Thus, there is a long history of attempts to assess privacy policies automatically. To name a prominent example, in 2004, the Platform for Privacy Preferences (P3P) [12] standardized a protocol, that allowed data controllers to publish machine-readable privacy policies. Web browser plug-ins such as the Privacy Bird [88] allowed users to specify their privacy preferences, which were automatically compared against P3P policies. However, websites were not obligated to use P3P, and the specification of meaningful preferences is a difficult task. Later approaches used NLP approaches such as morphological, lexical, syntactic, and semantic analyses or ontology reasoning to assess privacy policies (see [13] for a detailed comparison). For example [14], a support vector machine can be trained to map the sentences of a privacy policy to the mandatory information and user rights, that must be declared in a privacy policy. AI has also been used, e.g., to verify whether the content of a privacy policy is complete [15] [16] according to the GDPR. The advantage of such approaches is that they work without the help of data controllers. The work closest to ours is [17], which gauges the effectiveness of ChatGPT-4, Bard, and Bing AI for assessing privacy policies. This approach acknowledges the technical feasibility of such an assessment and provides quality measures, but leaves aside the impact of the prompt engineer and all ethical and legal issues.

III. Our Research Approach

To provide a systematic overview of ethical, legal, and technical challenges of letting an LLM assess privacy policies for the users, we pursued an explorative approach. This approach is the common basis of the respective research methods from our very different research disciplines, which enables us to combine our findings into an interdisciplinary result:

1) As a first step, we **compile an annotated bibliography** on LLMs and privacy policy assessment (cf. Sec. II). We also **implemented and tested a number of approaches** for assessing domain-specific texts with an LLM to gain first-hand experience, and discussed these in our research groups, e.g., [59] [89] [90] [91].
2) In a second step, we use this combination of background information and first-hand experience to **formulate a series of challenges** in the three pillars described.
3) Finally, we **filter for challenges** that are specific to our application domain, i.e., we exclude general difficulties in obtaining training data, performance, explainability, enforcement of legal norms for complex IT systems, etc.

In the following sections, we describe the challenges we have obtained using this approach.

IV. Technical Challenges

Our research groups have first-hand experience in investigating the transparency of German privacy policies [34]. We also investigated, to which extent LLMs can be used to assess and explain difficult security issues [89] or solve exam questions at Bachelor's or Master's level [92]. We also modeled privacy practices as structured design patterns [93] [94], the implementation quality of which can be estimated or measured. With a fairness certification for NLP and LLMs, we introduced criteria for addressing biases in the model output [95]. We also let an LLM assess multiple dimensions of fairness in privacy policies [59] [90]. Based on this hands-on experience and our literature base in Section II, we derive six technical challenges:

Interest in certain privacy policies is private data. When using an LLM to assess a privacy policy according to ethics, morale, legality etc., the users reveal their interests. Assume a user calls for an assessment of a privacy policy of an AI company, and expresses concerns due to personal data used as training data. This is sensitive information, which calls for anonymization or on-premise solutions.

Annotated data sets as a ground truth are limited. To enable few-shot prompting and fine-tuning of LLMs, as well as to enable a solid evaluation, annotated data sets with ground truths for policies are required. The closest to such a data set is TOSDR [96], which provides crowd-sourced / automatically generated annotations for popular policies. However, these annotations are limited in number and quality control.

The assessment requires individual prompts. LLMs need to incorporate user-specific preferences and concerns into their prompts to effectively assess privacy policies, accommodating various social and educational backgrounds. This includes fighting biased responses, ensuring the representation of diverse opinions. An interactive tool or a set of tailored prompt templates that can handle these nuances may be required.

Explaining the assessment to the user. Due to hallucinations of the LLM, the LLM misunderstanding a privacy policy, or a user misunderstanding the LLM assessment, mistakes might occur. It is an important challenge to structure an LLM approach for the assessment of privacy policies in a way that tolerates mistakes. For example, an interactive approach might allow the LLM to ask back for specific user preferences, which increases the user's awareness.

The data controller must not influence the assessment. Companies might utilize limitations regarding the robustness of an LLM-based ethics assessment to get more favorable assessments without improving their privacy practices. Targeted variations of their policies without changing their semantic content could be used to optimize for higher ratings. This makes testing robustness of the LLM output, and particularly adversarial testing of LLM assessments essential.

It needs strategies for consistent LLM assessments. The LLM assessment may depend on nuances in the prompt and the privacy policy, that a human would overlook, resulting in different assessments for similar privacy policies. This undermines the reliability and trustworthiness of generated assessments. Therefore, approaches for enforcing structure in outputs and optimizing the prompting in a way that is consistently followed by the LLM are important.

V. Ethical Challenges

Incorporating ethical analysis into an AI environment requires an operationalization of ethics with the aim of its mathematical implementation. We delved into concepts such as fairness in AI from a quantitative perspective [49]. We also analyzed the relationship between technology and ethics. In the era of AI, this relationship requires human oversight to avoid a blind and potentially misleading technization of otherwise qualitatively expressed goals [50]. With this in mind, we formulate four challenges:

Different stakeholders have different objectives. It is an open issue how to assess the dimensions of fairness for privacy policies: While the users should want to provide as little data as possible, the data controllers rely on data to further develop their services. It is challenging to identify a way to balance these objectives responsibly.

Identifying socially desirable practices. While legal regulations hint at what voters might want as they are results of law-making processes in representative democracies, it remains opaque, what is socially desirable. Thus, what would a set of data management practices look like that meet everyone's privacy needs, and can serve as a reference for assessing privacy policies?

Operationalizing the evaluative criteria. To identify a socially desirable outcome, methods are needed to operationalize evaluative criteria for the assessment of privacy policies. While the same setting might be judged as fair or unfair depending on the position of those who judge, a metric can objectively measure intersubjectively acceptable parameters. However, such parameters are unknown yet.

The status of the assessment must be defined. The LLM's assessment is meant to guide the user regarding the acceptability of a privacy policy. The output of the LLM is the product of intricate 'translation processes' [50], in which the quantitative elements ('scores') are expressed in words. It can be paternalism, if users take the LLM's assessment as their decision, narrowing down the user's autonomy. However, the LLM could be the only option to quickly assess privacy.

VI. Legal Challenges

Our previous research in fields such as transparency, trust, data protection, and responsibility when using AI in legally sensitive areas [97] has shown that, in particular, transparency and user trust are essential to ensure broad acceptance and fair use of AI technologies [98]. In addition, property rights, data protection [99] [24] and liability [100] must be clearly regulated and respected in the digital age to protect the rights of individuals. On this basis, we identified four challenges:

Common understanding of fairness and transparency. While Art. 12 of the GDPR requires privacy policies to be comprehensible and comprehensive to allow autonomous decisions, there is a lack of common understanding of fairness and transparency and how to achieve them. Navigating the AI era requires a clear understanding from all stakeholders [101]–[103]. New approaches are needed to prove lawful processing, i.e., to describe in clear language how the data is collected, pre-processed, used for training, which prompts and outputs are used, and whether training is carried out with outputs [104], mainly focusing on explainability [21].

Questionable validity of AI supported consent. Art. 7 GDPR requires the subject of data processing to make an informed and free decision. Using an AI tool as a support can, under certain circumstances, be seen as an influence jeopardising the validity of given consent. It becomes more questionable in case the AI tool is manipulative, which is prohibited by Art. 5 of the AI Act [4].

Compliance with the AI Act and related regulations. An AI tool to assess privacy policies can be considered a High-Risk AI System in the meaning of Art. 6 ff. AI Act [4] and therefore the provider, distributor, or deployer can be subject to extensive obligations. Depending on the specific use in a single case, it might also fall under the scope of the ePrivacy Directive [105] and its potentially varying national implementation acts, e.g., the German TDDDG [106].

Liability of the assessment is an open question. If users base their consent to the data practices of a data controller on the assessment by an AI tool, it is not clear who shall be liable in case of possible damages occurring on either side, e.g, the loss of control over personal data of the data subject or business losses of the data controller.

VII. Discussion

Using LLMs is a promising approach to analyzing privacy policies. LLMs can efficiently process numerous, lengthy privacy policies without getting tired, or losing focus and interest. This is a very practical feature, as every active Internet or smartphone user uses many different services every day, each of which has its own privacy policy. Furthermore, it might be possible to carefully instruct the LLM to produce assessments that are more consistent and objective than a human assessment. With suitable prompting techniques, it is also possible to individualize the assessment for different priorities of the users at a given time. As an example, it is possible to prompt the LLM for an assessment from a non-native person's point of view, which might include less complex words, and terminology. As the technology evolves a use by supervisory authorities to monitor compliance with the requirements of Art. 12 and 13 GDPR is conceivable.

However, existing LLMs are notorious for hallucinations. Reluctant service providers, who suspect that their customers are using LLM, might be tempted to write its privacy policy in a way that provokes such hallucinations, e.g., by using unusual phrases that were underrepresented in the training data of the LLM. In addition to these general limitations, we have identified a large number of different interdisciplinary challenges for an LLM-based assessment of privacy policies. Nevertheless, we think that it would be better to have an LLM reading privacy policies than a human who is too busy to read them at all as a preliminary step, and prevent potential privacy risks go unnoticed for sure. As human agency and oversight are key components of a trustworthy AI, it should be kept in mind that the LLM-based assessment of privacy policies aims to support the autonomous decision-making of the users to strengthen their fundamental right to privacy, not to replace the decision-making authority [21].

VIII. Conclusion

Effective privacy policies are essential for maintaining transparency in data usage and enabling users to assess privacy risks. However, the complexity and length of these policies can often lead to confusion and consent fatigue, where users might inadvertently agree to practices that are not in their best interest. To tackle these challenges, our study investigated the use of LLMs to automatically evaluate and simplify privacy policies. We explored the technical feasibility, ethical implications, and legal compatibility of using LLMs for this purpose. We aim to identify potential areas for further research and to stimulate a dialogue on how risk-based policies could be effectively shaped using LLM technology.

Employing large-scale language models to interpret and simplify privacy policies is a crucial and timely research endeavor. This interdisciplinary approach addressed the urgent need for transparency in AI-driven contexts and utilized the unique capabilities of LLMs to enhance user understanding and decision-making. By integrating legal expertise, advanced machine learning technologies, and considerations of ethical and societal impacts, our research aims to reduce consent fatigue, counter unfair data practices, and empower individuals in a digital age dominated by complex data interactions.

References

[1] K. Hu, "ChatGPT sets record fastest growing user base, analyst note," *Reuters*, 02 2023, retrieved: Aug. 2024. [Online]. Available: https://www.reuters.com/technology/chatgpt-sets-record-fastest-growing-user-base-analyst-note-2023-02-01/

[2] OpenAI, "GPT-4 turbo," 11 2023, retrieved: Aug. 2024. [Online]. Available: https://openai.com/blog/new-models-and-developer-products-announced-at-devday

[3] M. Chui, E. Hazan, R. Roberts, A. Singla, and K. Smaje, "The economic potential of generative AI," McKinsey Whitepaper, 2023.

[4] European Commission, "Proposal for a regulation of the european parliament and of the council laying down harmonized rules on artificial intelligence," CELEX:52021PC0206, 2021.

[5] European Union, "Regulation (EU) 2016/679 of the European Parliament and of the Council of 27 april 2016 on the protection of natural persons with regard to the processing of personal data and on the free movement of such data (General Data Protection Regulation)," *Official Journal of the European Union*, vol. L119/1, 2016.

[6] S. I. Becher and U. Benoliel, "Law in books and law in action: The readability of privacy policies and the GDPR," in *Consumer law and economics*. Springer, 2021, pp. 179–204.

[7] C. Warzel and N. Ash, "Google's 4,000-word privacy policy is a secret history of the internet," *The New York Times*, 2019.

[8] Y. Shvartzshnaider, N. Apthorpe, N. Feamster, and H. Nissenbaum, "Analyzing privacy policies using contextual integrity annotations," *arXiv preprint arXiv:1809.02236*, 2018.

[9] B. W. Schermer, B. Custers, and S. van der Hof, "The crisis of consent: How stronger legal protection may lead to weaker consent in data protection." *Ethics and Information Technology*, vol. 16, p. 171–182, 2014.

[10] C. McClain, M. Faverio, M. Anderson, and E. Park. (2023) How Americans view data privacy. Retrieved: Aug. 2024. [Online]. Available: https://www.pewresearch.org/internet/2023/10/18/how-americans-view-data-privacy/

[11] Cisco. (2019) Consumer privacy survey. Retrieved: Aug. 2024. [Online]. Available: https://www.cisco.com/c/dam/global/en_uk/products/collateral/security/cybersecurity-series-2019-cps.pdf

[12] W3C, "The platform for privacy preferences 1.1 (P3P1.1) specification publication history," https://www.w3.org/standards/history/P3P11/, retrieved: Aug. 2024.

[13] J. M. Del Alamo, D. S. Guaman, B. García, and A. Diez, "A systematic mapping study on automated analysis of privacy policies," *Computing*, vol. 104, no. 9, pp. 2053–2076, 2022.

[14] D. Sánchez, A. Viejo, and M. Batet, "Automatic assessment of privacy policies under the GDPR," *Applied Sciences*, vol. 11, no. 4, p. 1762, 2021.

[15] O. Amaral, S. Abualhaija, D. Torre, M. Sabetzadeh, and L. C. Briand, "AI-enabled automation for completeness checking of privacy policies," *IEEE Transactions on Software Engineering*, vol. 48, no. 11, pp. 4647–4674, 2021.

[16] D. Torre, S. Abualhaija, M. Sabetzadeh, L. Briand, K. Baetens, P. Goes, and S. Forastier, "An AI-assisted approach for checking the completeness of privacy policies against GDPR," in *2020 IEEE 28th International Requirements Engineering Conference (RE)*. IEEE, 2020, pp. 136–146.

[17] A. Hamid, H. R. Samidi, T. Finin, P. Pappachan, and R. Yus, "Genaipabench: A benchmark for generative AI-based privacy assistants," *arXiv preprint arXiv:2309.05138*, 2023.

[18] OpenAI, "GPT-4 technical report," *arXiv preprint arXiv:2303.08774*, 2023.

[19] G. Malgieri, "The concept of fairness in the GDPR: A linguistic and contextual interpretation," in *Proceedings of the 2020 Conference on fairness, accountability, and transparency*, 2020, pp. 154–166.

[20] European Commission, "Regulation (eu) 2022/2065 of the european parliament and of the council of 19 october 2022 on a single market for digital services and amending directive 2000/31/ec (digital services act)," *Official Journal of the European Union*, 2022.

[21] High-Level Expert Group on Artificial Intelligence, European Commission, "Ethics guidelines for Trustworthy AI," 2019.

[22] R. N. Zaeem and K. S. Barber, "The effect of the GDPR on privacy policies: Recent progress and future promise," *ACM Transactions on Management Information Systems*, vol. 12, no. 1, pp. 1–20, 2020.

[23] A. M. McDonald and L. F. Cranor, "The cost of reading privacy policies," *I/S: A Journal of Law and Policy for the Information Society*, vol. 4, p. 543, 2008.

[24] J. Möller-Klapperich, "Kunst, Kultur und Künstliche Intelligenz," in *Sicherheit und Recht im Wandel*. Cuvillier, 2023.

[25] A. Sattler, "Informationelle Privatautonomie," in *Jus Privatum 264, Mohr Siebeck*. Mohr Siebeck, 2022.

[26] L. F. Cranor, "Necessary but not sufficient: Standardized mechanisms for privacy notice and choice," *Journal on Telecommunications and High Technology Law*, vol. 10, pp. 273–308, 2012.

[27] U. Freiherr von Ulmenstein, "Datensouveränität durch repräsentative Rechtswahrnehmung," *DuD*, vol. 8, pp. 528–534, 2020.

[28] A. S. Chilton and O. Ben-Shahar, "Simplification of privacy disclosures: An experimental test," *Coase- Sandor Working Paper Series in Law and Economics*, vol. 737, pp. 41–67, 2016.

[29] J. Mainz, "An indirect argument for the access theory of privacy," *Res Publica*, vol. 27, no. 3, pp. 309–328, 2021.

[30] B. Lundgren, "A dilemma for privacy as control," *The Journal of Ethics*, vol. 24, no. 2, pp. 165–175, 2020.

[31] D. Elliott and E. Soifer, "AI technologies, privacy, and security," *Frontiers in Artificial Intelligence*, vol. 5, pp. 1–8, 2022.

[32] A. Marmor, "What is the right to privacy?" *Philosophy and Public Affairs*, vol. 43, p. 3, 2015.

[33] I. Harris, R. C. Jennings, D. Pullinger, S. Rogerson, and P. Duquenoy, "Ethical assessment of new technologies: a meta-methodology," *Journal of Information, Communication and Ethics in Society*, vol. 9, no. 1, pp. 49–64, 2011.

[34] B. Bartelt and E. Buchmann, "Transparency in privacy policies," in *12th International Conference on Building and Exploring Web Based Environments*, 2024.

[35] V. Belcheva, T. Ermakova, and B. Fabian, "Understanding website privacy policies — A longitudinal analysis using natural language processing," *Information*, vol. 14, no. 11, p. 622, 2023.

[36] J. R. Reidenberg *et al.*, "Disagreeable privacy policies: Mismatches between meaning and users' understanding," *Berkeley Tech. LJ*, vol. 30, p. 39, 2015.

[37] H. Choi, J. Park, and Y. Jung, "The role of privacy fatigue in online privacy behavior," *Computers in Human Behavior*, vol. 81, pp. 42–51, 2018.

[38] I. Pollach, "A typology of communicative strategies in online privacy policies: Ethics, power and informed consent," *Journal of Business Ethics*, vol. 62, pp. 221–235, 2005.

[39] J. Koetsier, "Viral app faceapp now owns access to more than 150 million people's faces and names," July 17 2019, retrieved: Aug. 2024. [Online]. Available: https://www.forbes.com/sites/johnkoetsier/2019/07/17/viral-app-faceapp-now-owns-access-to-more-than-150-million-peoples-faces-and-names/

[40] W. B. Tesfay, P. Hofmann, T. Nakamura, S. Kiyomoto, and J. Serna, "Privacyguide: Towards an implementation of the eu GDPR on internet privacy policy evaluation," in *Proceedings of the Fourth ACM International Workshop on Security and Privacy Analytics*, 2018, pp. 15–21.

[41] N. Zaeem *et al.*, "Privacycheck v2: A tool that recaps privacy policies for you," in *Proceedings of the 29th ACM International Conference on Information & Knowledge Management*, 2020, pp. 3441–3444.

[42] J. Wei *et al.*, "Emergent abilities of large language models," *arXiv preprint arXiv:2206.07682*, 2022.

[43] B. Guo, X. Zhang, Z. Wang, M. Jiang, J. Nie, Y. Ding, J. Yue, and Y. Wu, "How close is ChatGPT to human experts? Comparison corpus, evaluation, and detection," *arXiv preprint arXiv:2301.07597*, 2023.

[44] C. Tang *et al.*, "PolicyGPT: Automated analysis of privacy policies with large language models," *arXiv preprint arXiv:2309.10238*, 2023.

[45] P. Pałka, M. Lippi, F. Lagioia, R. Liepiņa, and G. Sartor, "No more trade-offs. GPT and fully informative privacy policies," *arXiv preprint arXiv:2402.00013*, 2023.

[46] J. W. DeCew, "The scope of privacy in law and ethics," *Law and Philosophy*, pp. 145–173, 1986.

[47] A. Acquisti, L. Brandimarte, and G. Loewenstein, "Privacy and human behavior in the age of information," *Science*, vol. 347, no. 6221, pp. 509–514, 2015.

[48] C. Véliz, *Privacy Is Power: Why and How You Should Take Back Control of Your Data*. Penguin Random House, 2020.

[49] C. Geldhauser and H. Diebel-Fischer, "Is diverse and inclusive AI trapped in the gap between reality and algorithmizability?" in *Northern Lights Deep Learning Conference*. PMLR, 2024, pp. 75–80.

[50] H. Diebel-Fischer, "Technisch realisierte Ethik? Anthropologische Perspektiven auf das Verhältnis von Technik und Ethik," in *Mensch und Maschine im Zeitalter der 'Künstlichen Intelligenz'*, H. Diebel-Fischer, N. Kunkel, and J. Zeyher-Quattlender, Eds. Lit, 2023, pp. 49–64.

[51] M. Huppenbauer, P. Kirchschläger, and G. Ulshöfer, *Digitalisierung aus theologischer und ethischer Perspektive. Konzeptionen - Anfragen - Impulse*. Nomos, 2021.

[52] C. Benn and S. Lazar, "What's wrong with automated influence," *Canadian Journal of Philosophy*, vol. 52, no. 1, pp. 125–148, 2022.

[53] J. P. Choi, D.-S. Jeon, and B.-C. Kim, "Privacy and personal data collection with information externalities," *Journal of Public Economics*, vol. 173, pp. 113–124, 2019.

[54] B. Platow, "Religion and the technology of digitization in education," in *Oxford Handbook of Religion and Education*, L. Gearon and A. Kuusisto, Eds. Oxford University Press, forthcoming, ch. 40.

[55] B. Platow, "Digitalisierung/Big Data/Künstliche Intelligenz," in *Ethische Kernthemen (Theologie für Lehrerinnen und Lehrer, Bd. 2)*, M. Rothgangel, H. Simojoki, and U. Körtner, Eds. Vandenhoeck & Ruprecht, 2021, pp. 85–95.

[56] J. Gogoll, N. Zuber, S. Kacianka, T. Greger, A. Pretschner, and J. Nida-Rümelin, "Ethics in the software development process: From codes of conduct to ethical deliberation," *Philosophy & Technology*, vol. 34, no. 4, pp. 1085–1108, 2021.

[57] S. Krügel, A. Ostermaier, and M. Uhl, "ChatGPT's inconsistent moral advice influences users' judgment," *Scientific Reports*, vol. 13, no. 1, p. 4569, 2023.

[58] M. Nauta, J. Trienes, S. Pathak, E. Nguyen, M. Peters, Y. Schmitt, J. Schlötterer, M. van Keulen, and C. Seifert, "From anecdotal evidence to quantitative evaluation methods: A systematic review on evaluating

explainable AI," *ACM Computing Surveys*, vol. 55, no. 13s, p. 1–42, 2023.
[59] V. Freiberger and E. Buchmann, "Legally binding but unfair? Towards assessing fairness of privacy policies," *arXiv preprint arXiv:2403.08115*, 2024.
[60] T. Hagendorff, "Machine psychology: Investigating emergent capabilities and behavior in large language models using psychological methods," *arXiv preprint arXiv:2303.13988*, 2023.
[61] J. Achiam *et al.*, "GPT-4 technical report," *arXiv preprint arXiv:2303.08774*, 2023.
[62] J. L. Espejel, E. H. Ettifouri, M. S. Y. Alassan, E. M. Chouham, and W. Dahhane, "GPT-3.5, GPT-4, or BARD? Evaluating LLMs reasoning ability in zero-shot setting and performance boosting through prompts," *Natural Language Processing Journal*, vol. 5, p. 100032, 2023.
[63] S. Bubeck *et al.*, "Sparks of artificial general intelligence: Early experiments with GPT-4," *arXiv preprint arXiv:2303.12712*, 2023.
[64] J. W. Rae *et al.*, "Scaling language models: Methods, analysis & insights from training gopher," *arXiv preprint arXiv:2112.11446*, 2021.
[65] T. Kojima, S. S. Gu, M. Reid, Y. Matsuo, and Y. Iwasawa, "Large language models are zero-shot reasoners," *Advances in neural information processing systems*, vol. 35, pp. 22 199–22 213, 2022.
[66] J. Wei *et al.*, "Chain-of-thought prompting elicits reasoning in large language models," *Advances in Neural Information Processing Systems*, vol. 35, pp. 24 824–24 837, 2022.
[67] T. Brown *et al.*, "Language models are few-shot learners," *Advances in neural information processing systems*, vol. 33, pp. 1877–1901, 2020.
[68] S. Yao, D. Yu, J. Zhao, I. Shafran, T. Griffiths, Y. Cao, and K. Narasimhan, "Tree of thoughts: Deliberate problem solving with large language models," in *Proceedings of Advances in Neural Information Processing Systems (NeurIPS 2023)*, 2023.
[69] Y. Zhou, A. I. Muresanu, Z. Han, K. Paster, S. Pitis, H. Chan, and J. Ba, "Large language models are human-level prompt engineers," *arXiv preprint arXiv:2211.01910*, 2022.
[70] P. Liu, W. Yuan, J. Fu, Z. Jiang, H. Hayashi, and G. Neubig, "Pre-train, prompt, and predict: A systematic survey of prompting methods in natural language processing," *ACM Computing Surveys*, vol. 55, no. 9, pp. 1–35, 2023.
[71] G. Kim, P. Baldi, and S. McAleer, "Language models can solve computer tasks," in *Proceedings of Advances in Neural Information Processing Systems (NeurIPS 2023)*, 2023.
[72] J. Zamfirescu-Pereira, R. Y. Wong, B. Hartmann, and Q. Yang, "Why Johnny can't prompt: How non-AI experts try (and fail) to design LLM prompts," in *Proceedings of the 2023 CHI Conference on Human Factors in Computing Systems*, 2023, pp. 1–21.
[73] E. Lee, "Control openai model behavior with seed: Step-by-step with code," https://drlee.io/control-openai-model-behavior-with-seed-step-by-step-with-code-9bba4e137a63, 01 2024, retrieved: Aug. 2024.
[74] Z. Jiang, F. F. Xu, J. Araki, and G. Neubig, "How can we know what language models know?" *Transactions of the Association for Computational Linguistics*, vol. 8, pp. 423–438, 2020.
[75] W. Yuan, G. Neubig, and P. Liu, "Bartscore: Evaluating generated text as text generation," *Advances in Neural Information Processing Systems*, vol. 34, pp. 27 263–27 277, 2021.
[76] M. Martinc, S. Pollak, and M. Robnik-Šikonja, "Supervised and unsupervised neural approaches to text readability," *Computational Linguistics*, vol. 47, no. 1, pp. 141–179, 2021.
[77] W. Dubay, "The principles of readability," *CA*, vol. 92627949, pp. 631–3309, 01 2004.
[78] G. Robert, *The Technique of Clear Writing*. McGraw-Hill; Revised edition, 1968.
[79] J. P. Kincaid, R. P. Fishburne Jr, R. L. Rogers, and B. S. Chissom, "Derivation of new readability formulas for navy enlisted personnel," Naval Technical Training Command Millington, Tech. Rep., 1975.
[80] G. H. Mc Laughlin, "Smog grading-a new readability formula," *Journal of reading*, vol. 12, no. 8, pp. 639–646, 1969.
[81] S. A. Crossley, S. Skalicky, M. Dascalu, D. S. McNamara, and K. Kyle, "Predicting text comprehension, processing, and familiarity in adult readers: New approaches to readability formulas," *Discourse Processes*, vol. 54, no. 5-6, pp. 340–359, 2017.
[82] J. Hancke, S. Vajjala, and D. Meurers, "Readability classification for German using lexical, syntactic, and morphological features," in *Proceedings of COLING 2012*, Dec. 2012, pp. 1063–1080.
[83] P. G. Blaneck, T. Bornheim, N. Grieger, and S. Bialonski, "Automatic readability assessment of German sentences with transformer ensembles," in *Proceedings of the GermEval 2022 Workshop on Text Complexity Assessment of German Text*, Potsdam, Germany, 2022.
[84] T. vor der Brück and S. Hartrumpf, "A semantically oriented readability checker for german," 2007, pp. 270–274.
[85] F. Pickelmann, M. Färber, and A. Jatowt, "Ablesbarkeitsmesser: A system for assessing the readability of german text," in *Advances in Information Retrieval - 45th European Conference on Information Retrieval, ECIR 2023, Dublin, Ireland, April 2-6, 2023, Proceedings, Part III*, ser. Lecture Notes in Computer Science, vol. 13982. Springer, 2023, pp. 288–293.
[86] O. Guhr, A.-K. Schumann, F. Bahrmann, and H. J. Böhme, "Training a broad-coverage German sentiment classification model for dialog systems," in *Proceedings of The 12th Language Resources and Evaluation Conference*, 2020, pp. 1620–1625.
[87] M. Färber, V. Burkard, A. Jatowt, and S. Lim, "A multidimensional dataset based on crowdsourcing for analyzing and detecting news bias," in *29th ACM International Conference on Information and Knowledge Management*, 2020, pp. 3007–3014.
[88] L. F. Cranor, "P3P: Making privacy policies more useful," *IEEE Security & Privacy*, vol. 1, no. 6, pp. 50–55, 2003.
[89] V. Jüttner, M. Grimmer, and E. Buchmann, "Chatids: Explainable cybersecurity using generative ai," in *Proceedings of the 17th International Conference on Emerging Security Information, Systems and Technologies (SECURWARE'23)*, 2023.
[90] V. Freiberger and E. Buchmann, "Fair balancing? evaluating llm-based privacy policy ethics assessments," in *Proceedings of the 3rd European Workshop on Algorithmic Fairness (EWAF'24)*, 2024.
[91] M. Hoffmann and E. Buchmann, "Chatsec: Spicing up vulnerability scans with ai for heterogeneous university it - towards enhancing security vulnerability reports for non-experts," in *Proceedings of the 1st International Conference on AI-based Systems and Services (AISyS'24)*, 2024.
[92] E. Buchmann and A. Thor, "Online exams in the era of ChatGPT," in *Tagungsband der 21. Fachtagung Bildungstechnologien der GI Fachgruppe Bildungstechnologien (DELFI 2023)*, 2023.
[93] M. Robak and E. Buchmann, "Deriving workflow privacy patterns from legal documents," in *Proceedings of the 14th Federated Conference on Computer Science and Information Systems (FedCSIS'19)*, 2019.
[94] M. Robak and E. Buchmann, "How to extract workflow privacy patterns from legal documents," in *Proceedings of the 17th Conference on Advanced Information Technologies for Management (AITM'19)*, 2019.
[95] V. Freiberger and E. Buchmann, "Fairness certification for natural language processing and large language models," in *Proceedings of the 10th Intelligent Systems Conference (IntelliSys'24)*, 2024.
[96] ToS;DR, "Terms of service; didn't read," https://tosdr.org/, retrieved: Aug. 2024.
[97] J. Möller-Klapperich, "ChatGPT und Co. - aus der Perspektive der Rechtswissenschaft," *Neue Justiz*, vol. 4, 2023.
[98] A. Lauber-Rönsberg, "Transparency by Design als Rechtsprinzip gegen Dark Patterns," in *Künstliche Intelligenz: wie gelingt eine vertrauenswürdige Verwendung in Deutschland und Europa?* Mohr Siebeck, 2022.
[99] A. Lauber-Rönsberg, "BDSG und andere sondergesetzliche Datenschutzregelungen," in *Handbuch europäisches und deutsches Datenschutzrecht*, 2019.
[100] J. Möller-Klapperich and C. Rasquin, "Regulatorische Herausforderungen in KI-Wertschöpfungsketten," *Neue Justiz*, vol. 10, 2023.
[101] European Data Protection Board, "Guidelines no. 4/2019 on article 25 data protection by design and default," 2020.
[102] European Data Protection Supervisor, "Opinion 5/2018. preliminary opinion on privacy by design," 2018.
[103] European Union Agency for Network and Information Security, "Privacy and data protection by design – from policy to engineering," 2015.
[104] European Data Protection Board, "Report of the work undertaken by the ChatGPT taskforce," 2024.
[105] European Commission, "Directive 2002/58/EC of the european parliament and of the council of 12 july 2002 concerning the processing of personal data and the protection of privacy in the electronic communications sector (directive on privacy and electronic communications)," *Official Journal of the European Union*, 2020.
[106] Bundesrepublik Deutschland, "Telekommunikation-Digitale-Dienste-Datenschutz-Gesetz (TDDDG)," *Bundesgesetzblatt 2024 I Nr. 149*, 2024.

Combining Templates and Language Models for the Automatic Creation of Scientific Overviews

Sarah Frank
CERN, Switzerland
Institute of Information Systems and Data Science
Graz University of Technology, Austria
e-mail: sarah.frank@cern.ch

Andreas Wagner
CERN, Switzerland

Christian Guetl
Institute of Information Systems
and Data Science
Graz University of Technology, Austria

Abstract—**The number of scientific publications is increasing at a rate that makes them progressively more impossible to keep up with. Consequently, automatic creation of summaries from a collection of articles could significantly speed up the selection of publications of interest. This paper focuses on the use case of ultra-short summaries to be used for the creation of topic overviews, as often found in journal editorials. We used a combination of a pre-trained language model and templates to create a coherent text summarizing the papers contained within single journal issues. Following this, we conducted two user studies. The results were generally promising, with users preferring the automatically created summary in a majority of cases. Evaluations of the accuracy, coverage, fluency, and informativeness of the summaries showed that most users found them to be good. However, the variation in the evaluation scores was significant both by user and summary. Text quality was shown to be graded differently according to the user's requirements and familiarity with the typical form of this kind of summary. Furthermore, the importance of high-quality base summaries from the language model, as well as a high number of available templates, cannot be overstated.**

Keywords-automatic summarization; hybrid summarization; language models; natural language processing; templates.

I. Introduction

As new information is generated at an increasingly fast pace, automatic summarization has the potential to support a variety of daily tasks. Despite rapid improvements in the field of NLP (Natural Language Processing), including the creation of large language models, common issues with the generated texts remain. Hallucination, that is, the generation of information that is not supported by the input text, can lead to results that misrepresent statements or are completely false in relation to the input data. Furthermore, the lack of explainability of many existing models leads to difficulties when trying to trace a piece of information back to its source [1]. The particular importance of the information to remain consistent with the source text in scientific environments suggests that current transformer-based solutions often do not meet usability requirements [2].

Before transformers were introduced in 2017, automatic summarisation relied on a variety of different methods such as statistical measures [3], graph-based methods [4][5], and templates [6]–[9]. Template-based summarisation methods, in particular, provide a structured framework for text generation that can enforce certain sentence structures, incorporate domain-specific knowledge, or fulfill given form requirements. Although template-based approaches on their own have disadvantages such as lack of flexibility, previous research has combined them with other methods such as transformers for named entity recognition [10] and general encoder/decoder architecture for electronic direct mail subject generation [11], fine-tuning language models [12], and template-aware summary rewriting [13].

Despite a variety of domains that have utilized templates for improved results, automatic summarization of scientific articles has so far not placed a focus on the approach. With new research being published at a rapid pace, tools that summarize a collection of papers may save a considerable amount of time. The combination of templates with transformer models has the potential to create well-formulated summaries that follow a given structure. This makes it an ideal approach for creating overviews of scientific papers, where a consistent layout is often present.

With the aim to use language models in combination with template-based summarization to create scientific structured text, this research aims to create well-formulated summaries that follow a given structure. Summaries of this kind could then be used to create an overview text of multiple scientific papers. The possibility of receiving regular summaries of recently published papers in a particular field of interest would allow researchers to stay up-to-date on current findings without actively having to search for information. In particular, our goal is to create summaries that can be utilized to give users a brief idea of the topic of a paper for use in editorials, on websites, or in newsletters.

In this paper, we evaluate the effect of combining transformer-model-created summaries with templates. The idea is to use this approach to automatically create overviews of multiple papers, including titles, author information, and short summaries within one sentence each. Texts such as these can, for example, find application as editorial summaries, which are often found in special issues of journals. Due to the lack of a suitable dataset for testing and evaluation of the resulting method, we created a test dataset consisting of 13 special issues comprised of 69 papers, collectively. We then evaluated a selection of language models for their single-sentence summaries using these scientific articles. With this approach, it is possible to retain source knowledge for the information given in the summaries, which is particularly important in scientific environments. Furthermore, the use of templates allows for the adaptation of the summary structure to the specific use case. Finally, this approach simplifies the evaluation of the factual accuracy of the summary in relation to the source text, as the reference document for each short summary is known.

To this end, our aim is to answer the following research questions (RQs):

- **RQ1:** How do existing language models perform when evaluated for the creation of ultra-short summaries?
- **RQ2:** How can templates tailor results for formulaic texts, such as journal editorials, when used in combination with transformer models?
- **RQ3:** How do the resulting summaries perform when evaluated for language and content quality by automatic and manual means?

In Section 2, we will first give an overview of the background of this work, such as automatic summarization and its importance in general, relevant datasets, and evaluation metrics, followed by an elaboration of works utilizing a combination of transformer- and template-based methods. This is followed by Section 3, which gives an explanation of the general approach and development stages, as well as details the implementation. Subsequently, Section 4 presents the results from both the automatic and manual evaluation methods. Finally, Section 5 discusses the findings and their meaning, and Section 6 finishes the paper by detailing possible limitations and future work.

II. Background and Related Work

The development of automatic summarization techniques has gained significant attention due to its wide range of potential applications. This is due in large part to the creation of transformer-based models [14] and the subsequent popularization of LLMs (Large Language Models), of which GPT (Generative Pre-trained Transformer) [15] and BERT (Bidirectional Encoder Representations from Transformers) [16] are arguably among the most well known. The disadvantage of these approaches is that the results are prone to hallucination, which is the generation of information that is not supported by the source material [17]. Even state-of-the-art models had hallucination-based errors in up to 25% of their summaries when [18] evaluated their correctness in 2019. Despite the fact that numerous attempts have been made to solve this problem since [17], hallucination remains a common issue. Ensuring the production of accurate and coherent summaries that capture the essential meaning of the source text remains a complex task [19]. Transformer-based approaches in particular face challenges related to explainability [20], ambiguity [21][22], redundancy [23][24], and avoiding biases [25][26].

Template-based summarization uses predefined patterns or templates for the generation process. These templates specify how the information from the source text should be organized in the summary and can be designed to capture specific types of information, such as key facts, main ideas, supporting evidence, or other relevant elements depending on the domain. One of the main advantages of this approach is its transparency; the use of fixed templates provides an explicit framework for summarization, which allows the resulting summary to remain explainable [27]. Template-based summarization, which is inherently rigid in its utilisation, can be particularly useful in domains where the structure of information is consistent across documents. Ambiguity, variations in writing styles, and changes in document structure can pose challenges. Furthermore, although the potential for domain-specific customization allows the design of templates that align with the specific needs of a particular use case, this need for domain-specific templates also has a limiting effect [28].

Due to their various advantages and disadvantages, NLP research regularly combines different methods to optimize results. In recent years, there has been an increasing interest in combining template-based summarization, in particular, with other techniques such as pre-trained language models and sentiment analysis [12][11][29][30]. Due to this, templates have also been combined with these methods more frequently, with some approaches specifically making use of pre-trained models such as BERT, and others adding additional pre-training or different attention mechanism. With an aim similar to that of this work in a different domain, Bilal et al. used the combination of templates, sentiment analysis, and abstractive summarization to summarize the opinions of microblogs [29].

Although research into the use of templates as a means of guiding summaries has spanned a variety of domains, research considering hybrid solutions involving templates is underrepresented for tasks including scientific articles.

III. Methods and Implementation

For the creation of the summary, the process was split into multiple stages. This included the creation of a test dataset due to the need for specific metadata and reference summaries of the journal issues as found in the editorials.

The test dataset was made up of 7 issues of "The Journal of Universal Computer Science", totaling 39 papers. The number of articles per issue varied, as seen in Table I. Each of the papers was pre-processed using GROBID and selected data extracted and saved in JSON format.

TABLE I
Overview of the number of articles contained in the issues, with issues being coded in the form of "volume/number"

Issue	26/07	26/09	26/10	26/11	27/01	28/03	28/10
# articles	4	9	4	8	3	6	5

In the next step, it was necessary to evaluate existing approaches that utilize language models. The summary created in this first stage presents the informational core that is later used to fill the templates. The quality of these subsummaries directly influences the quality of the final issue summary.

For the selection of the models, several conditions were formulated:

- The evaluated models are trained - and later tested - on scientific articles.
- The summary length is one or two sentences, with the result reflecting the overall topic of the article.

- Full sentence summaries are preferred to text fragments only.
- Abstractive single-document summarization

Several models that matched the requirements were evaluated for their performance. As each document was summarized by itself, the focus was on single-document abstractive summarization. The ones considered were LexRank [4], SciTLDR [31], Samsum [32], Pegasus-Pubmed [33], and LongT5 [34]. SciTLDR was used in three different ways: SciTLDR-F used the full text of the article to create the summary, SciTLDR-A used only the abstract, and SciTLDR-AC used the abstract and conclusion.

For an automatic evaluation of readability and complexity, the Python library textstat was used, in particular the Flesch reading ease score [35] and the automated readability index [36]. The Flesch reading ease score typically goes from (below) zero to 100, where lower scores signify higher difficulty, and higher scores easier texts. The automated readability index allocates a grade level to the text, with decimal numbers placing the text in-between two levels. A score of 14 is considered to indicate college-level literature.

Although these scores are typically used to assess the readability of longer literary texts, the choice was made to use them for the selection of the summarization model with the (much shorter) automatically created summaries. As they do not require a reference text to compare against (unlike ROUGE scores), their use was meant to give an indication of text quality and help with the selection of a promising model that returns an easily readable summary. The calculated scores are listed in Table II.

TABLE II
SELECTED LANGUAGE MODELS AND THEIR EVALUATION SCORES IN COMPARISON TO THE REFERENCE SUMMARY

Method	Metric			
	Flesch	Readability	ROUGE-1	ROUGE-L
Reference summary	25.20	20.28	-	-
SciTLDR-F	14.98	25.25	0.6402	0.4707
SciTLDR-A	11.79	26.10	0.6994	0.5713
SciTLDR-AC	6.66	26.91	0.6915	0.5667
LexRank	10.47	29.37	0.5343	0.3756
LongT5	40.89	13.87	0.2337	0.1710
Pegasus-Pubmed	44.33	14.24	0.2393	0.1786
Samsum	28.74	18.35	0.5026	0.4065
T5-one-line	14.78	24.68	0.6794	0.5244

In addition, both ROUGE-1 and ROUGE-L scores were calculated by comparing the automatically created sample summaries to the reference summary, to obtain further information on the performance of the model for this task. Taking into account the different evaluation metrics, the final decision was made according to the ROUGE scores. Flesch and Readability scores are intended to grade readability of text; as shorter sentences are usually considered to have better readability, partial summaries, although not matching the requirements, tended to perform better for these metrics.

The results showed a strong variation, with ROUGE-L scores between 0.1525 and 0.5556. SciTLDR [31], in particular SciTLDR-A, which used only the abstract as input, was found to work best for the intended purpose. Due to the intended short length of the summary, even creating one-sentence summaries leads to generally well-formed, informative results.

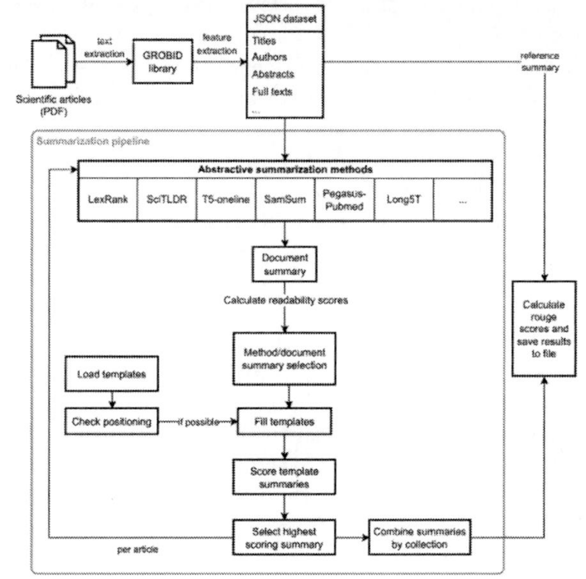

Figure 1. System architecture from PDFs to the final file containing all issue summaries.

The editorials are created using three general steps, with the process visualized in Figure 1: short document summary creation through an abstractive method, the use of templates to complete the summaries according to the pattern present in existing editorials, and post-processing through the use of the natural language toolkit.

The templates are selected according to specified criteria. Each template contains a placement array of the form [x, y, z], where each letter can take the value of 0 or 1, respectively. As an example, the template file of the sentence "Finally, in "[TITLE]", [AUTHORS] [SUMMARY]." contains the placement array [0,0,1], which means that it cannot be placed at the beginning or in the middle of a text. The only valid placement is at the end. This process is included as "Check positioning" in Figure 1. After non-applicable templates are discarded, candidate summaries are created using all remaining templates by combining them with the previously created short summary. These candidate template summaries are scored using the python package *textstat*'s method *text_standard* to evaluate readability. The candidate summary with the highest readability is then selected and combined with all other paper summaries from a specific journal issue.

The resulting summaries are evaluated both by automated means and manually by experts. For automatic evaluation, both ROUGE-1 and ROUGE-L are used.

For manual evaluation, two user studies were conducted for manual evaluation by experts. Each of them placed focus on a different aspect. The first compared the created summaries of articles with their equivalents from the reference summary and asked the evaluating person to choose the one they preferred overall.

For the second survey, participants received the abstract of an article and its respective automatically created summary. A five-point Likert scale was created to investigate how metrics such as fluency, informativeness, coverage, and accuracy were rated when put in context of the article's abstract.

The combination of both evaluations allowed insight into user preferences and aspects of particular focus.

IV. Results

When scoring the issue summaries using ROUGE-1 and ROUGE-L, the results showed an occasional strong variance, as visible in Table III. One particularly high score was an outlier, while there is no exceptionally low score. Overall, the results are promising but do suggest that it is necessary to pay particular attention to ensuring higher consistency in results to avoid outliers in any direction - though particularly lower scores.

TABLE III
ROUGE scores for each issue, comparing automatic issue summary to manually created reference summary.

Issue	ROUGE-1	ROUGE-L
26/07	0.91	0.73
26/09	0.68	0.53
26/10	0.60	0.53
26/11	0.77	0.64
27/01	0.64	0.49
28/03	0.63	0.42
28/10	0.70	0.56

The manual evaluation took place using two user surveys. Although only completed by a small number of participants, the results are important for future research directions and evaluations in which particular strengths and weaknesses of this approach can be found.

The first survey was started by 11 participants, with 8 of them completing it. The second survey was started by 14 participants and completed by 8, as well. In both cases, incomplete survey results were removed from the evaluation.

For the first survey, in which they noted their preference for either the automatically created summary or the manually created one, in 11 cases, the automatically created summary was preferred. In three cases, the votes were split equally between the two choices. In one notable case, all participants agreed and preferred the manual summary. Upon closer inspection, the automatically created summary was not grammatically correct.

In the second survey, 10 questions asked participants to rate each of the automatically created summaries on four metrics. The overall results were promising, though with a high standard deviation for coverage, fluency, and informativeness, as can be seen in Table IV. Optional free-text answers were given in a minority of cases, but allowed insight into the differing opinions of users that influenced the ratings positively as well as negatively.

TABLE IV
Performance evaluation for each of the given metrics, as well as average score and standard deviation (where "Very Poor" is 1 and "Excellent" is 5

Performance	Accuracy	Coverage	Fluency	Informativeness
Excellent	18	14	23	17
Good	48	35	28	32
Fair	11	13	18	19
Poor	2	16	10	10
Very Poor	1	2	1	2
Average	4	3.54	3.78	3.65
Std. Dev.	0.76	1.07	1.04	1.03

V. Discussion

The results did not suggest a relationship between the number of articles/subsummaries and the ROUGE score calculated for the overall issue summary. For example, both the highest and lowest ROUGE-1 scores were reached by issues that contained 4 articles (26/07 and 26/10). The highest ROUGE-L score was also scored by 26/07, with the lowest being 26/03, made up of 6 articles. Both 26/09 and 26/10 scored close ROUGE-L scores, with the first containing 9 articles and the second containing 4. Therefore, it does not appear that there is significant correlation to be found.

The survey invitations were sent to people in the academic field at a variety of levels of education, from bachelor's students to professors. The answers given - in particular the free-text answers in survey 2 - mirror the different levels of expectations the participants have for scientific summaries. While some participants paid particular attention to how fluently readable a summary was ("The repetition of full names is entirely irrelevant. It makes the sentences VERY hard to read[...]", others paid detailed attention to the wording and commonly used phrases ("Nice! Though it is a run-on sentence. May need a period there to separate it [...]"). Depending on the summary, participants either preferred summaries that were less detailed and more readable ("#2 gives more information but without any context it's hard to understand, #1 is more general" or preferred more detail ("The second summary is more detailed and fits better to the abstract", "Both summaries are of high quality, but #1 just seems to offer a more rounded and comprehensive snapshot of the abstract [...]").

Overall, the average performance of the summary was rated between "Fair" to "Good"; however, it becomes clear that the process is not reliable enough with respect to its output. Although most results are acceptable, there are instances where the summarization process fails to produce a grammatically correct sentence. In the test data, this was the case with one subsummary. In direct comparison to the manually created reference summary, all survey participants considered the automatically created summary sentence inadequate and preferred the reference summary.

The following summaries of a paper included in the test data illustrates this issue [37]:

"Damjan Fujs, Simon Vrhovec and Damjan Vavpotič present

"Bibliometric Mapping of Research on User Training for Secure Use of Information Systems", which conducted bibliometric mapping of research on user training for secure use of information systems."

This summary of the paper was automatically created. It is apparent that the first half of the sentence does not fit well with the second, as it appears that the article itself conducted the mapping instead of the authors. In comparison to the following summary, which was written by the issue's editors in the editorial, the automatically created summary clearly fails to measure up.

"In their paper "Bibliometric Mapping of Research on User Training for Secure Use of Information Systems, Damjan Fujs, Simon Vrhovec and Damjan Vavpotič conduct a bibliometric mapping of research on user training for secure use of information systems [38]."

For use in science, it is thus necessary to further extend or modify the approach explained in this paper to ensure correct grammar of summaries and consistent text quality, as anything less is likely to leave behind unsatisfied users.

VI. Conclusion and Future Work

This paper described an approach for the automatic summarization of scientific articles to create topic overviews. The combination of templates and language models led to results that were overall promising. Two user studies allowed showed where participants found strengths and weaknesses in the automatically created summaries, both compared to a manually created alternative, and when evaluated for specific metrics. The significant standard deviation in score indicates that the target audience should be strongly considered when creating a system such as this. Furthermore, the use of templates is problematic in combination with full sentences that do not necessarily follow a specific grammatical structure. As visible in one result, if a summary sentence is created that was not considered during the creation of the templates, it may lead to grammatically incorrect results that negatively impact the user experience.

Future work may consider the dynamic creation of templates, such as the use of a language model to create a larger variety than is feasible by hand. This would also solve the issue of repetitive sentence structures.

Furthermore, more language models should be considered for use in the future. Due to the constant development in the field, new models constantly appear. It may also be of interest to fine-tune an own model for either the creation of single-sentence summaries or templates.

Finally, it may be useful to increase each sub-summary length according to user preference. A user study may be useful to find the preferred summary length for specific use-cases, in which case a system that allows dynamic selection of sub-summary lengths might be a promising approach.

References

[1] A. Holzinger, A. Saranti, C. Molnar, P. Biecek, and W. Samek, "Explainable AI methods - a brief overview", in *xxAI - Beyond Explainable AI*, Springer International Publishing, 2022, pp. 13–38. DOI: 10.1007/978-3-031-04083-2_2.

[2] J. DeYoung, I. Beltagy, M. van Zuylen, B. Kuehl, and L. L. Wang, "MS^2: A dataset for multi-document summarization of medical studies", *Proceedings of the 2021 Conference on Empirical Methods in Natural Language Processing*, pp. 7494–7513, 2021. DOI: 10.18653/v1/2021.emnlp-main.594.

[3] H. P. Luhn, "The automatic creation of literature abstracts", *IBM Journal of Research and Development*, vol. 2, no. 2, pp. 159–165, 1958. DOI: 10.1147/rd.22.0159.

[4] G. Erkan and D. R. Radev, "LexRank: Graph-based lexical centrality as salience in text summarization", *Journal of Artificial Intelligence Research*, vol. 22, pp. 457–479, 2004. DOI: 10.1613/jair.1523.

[5] S. Beliga, A. Meštrović, and S. Martincic-Ipsic, "An overview of graph-based keyword extraction methods and approaches", *Journal of Information and Organizational Sciences*, vol. 39, pp. 1–20, 2015.

[6] S. M. Harabagiu and F. Lacatusu, "Generating single and multi-document summaries with gistexter", in *Document Understanding Conferences*, 2002, pp. 11–12.

[7] Y. Han, F. Li, K. Liu, and L. Liu, "Template based chinese news event summarization", in *Proceedings of the Second International Conference on Semantics, Knowledge, and Grid (SKG'06)*, IEEE, 2006. DOI: 10.1109/skg.2006.102.

[8] T. Oya, Y. Mehdad, G. Carenini, and R. Ng, "A template-based abstractive meeting summarization: Leveraging summary and source text relationships", in *Proceedings of the 8th International Natural Language Generation Conference (INLG)*, Association for Computational Linguistics, 2014, pp. 45–53. DOI: 10.3115/v1/w14-4407.

[9] P. G. Desai, H. Sarojadevi, and N. N. Chiplunkar, "A Template Based Algorithm for Automatic Summarization and Dialogue Management for Text Documents", *International Journal of Research in Engineering and Technology*, vol. 04, no. 11, pp. 334–340, 2015. DOI: 10.15623/ijret.2015.0411059.

[10] L. Cui, Y. Wu, J. Liu, S. Yang, and Y. Zhang, "Template-based named entity recognition using BART", in *Findings of the Association for Computational Linguistics: ACL-IJCNLP 2021*, Association for Computational Linguistics, 2021, pp. 1835–1845. DOI: 10.18653/v1/2021.findings-acl.161.

[11] Y.-H. Chen, P.-Y. Chen, H.-H. Shuai, and W.-C. Peng, "TemPEST: Soft template-based personalized EDM subject generation through collaborative summarization", *Proceedings of the AAAI Conference on Artificial Intelligence*, vol. 34, no. 05, pp. 7538–7545, 2020. DOI: 10.1609/aaai.v34i05.6252.

[12] K. Wang, X. Quan, and R. Wang, "BiSET: Bi-directional selective encoding with template for abstractive summarization", in *Proceedings of the 57th Annual Meeting of the Association for Computational Linguistics*, Association for Computational Linguistics, 2019, pp. 2153–2162. DOI: 10.18653/v1/P19-1207.

[13] Z. Cao, W. Li, S. Li, and F. Wei, "Retrieve, Rerank and Rewrite: Soft Template Based Neural Summarization", in *Proceedings of the 56th Annual Meeting of the Association for Computational Linguistics (Volume 1: Long Papers)*, Association for Computational Linguistics, 2018, pp. 152–161. DOI: 10.18653/v1/p18-1015.

[14] A. Vaswani *et al.*, "Attention is all you need", in *Advances in Neural Information Processing Systems*, vol. 30, Neural Information Processing Systems Foundation, Inc. (NeurIPS), 2017, pp. 5999–6009.

[15] A. Radford, K. Narasimhan, T. Salimans, and I. Sutskever, "Improving language understanding by generative pre-training",

2018, [Online]. Available: https://cdn.openai.com/research-covers/language-unsupervised/language_understanding_paper.pdf (visited on 08/29/2024).

[16] J. Devlin, M.-W. Chang, K. Lee, and K. Toutanova, "BERT: Pre-training of Deep Bidirectional Transformers for Language Understanding", in *Proceedings of the 2019 Conference of the North American Chapter of the Association for Computational Linguistics: Human Language Technologies*, vol. 1, Association for Computational Linguistics, 2019, pp. 4171–4186. DOI: 10.18653/v1/n19-1423.

[17] Z. Ji *et al.*, "Survey of hallucination in natural language generation", *ACM Computing Surveys*, vol. 55, no. 12, pp. 1–38, 2023. DOI: 10.1145/3571730.

[18] T. Falke, L. F. R. Ribeiro, P. A. Utama, I. Dagan, and I. Gurevych, "Ranking generated summaries by correctness: An interesting but challenging application for natural language inference", in *Proceedings of the 57th Annual Meeting of the Association for Computational Linguistics*, Association for Computational Linguistics, 2019, pp. 2214–2220. DOI: 10.18653/v1/p19-1213.

[19] J. Maynez, S. Narayan, B. Bohnet, and R. McDonald, "On faithfulness and factuality in abstractive summarization", in *Proceedings of the 58th Annual Meeting of the Association for Computational Linguistics*, Association for Computational Linguistics, 2020, pp. 1906–1919. DOI: 10.18653/v1/2020.acl-main.173.

[20] H. Wang, Y. Gao, Y. Bai, M. Lapata, and H. Huang, "Exploring explainable selection to control abstractive summarization", *Proceedings of the AAAI Conference on Artificial Intelligence*, vol. 35, no. 15, pp. 13 933–13 941, 2021. DOI: 10.1609/aaai.v35i15.17641.

[21] S. Jusoh, "A study on nlp applications and ambiguity problems", *Journal of Theoretical & Applied Information Technology*, vol. 96, no. 6, pp. 1486–1499, 2018.

[22] B. P. Yap, A. Koh, and E. S. Chng, "Adapting BERT for word sense disambiguation with gloss selection objective and example sentences", in *Findings of the Association for Computational Linguistics: EMNLP 2020*, Association for Computational Linguistics, 2020, pp. 41–46. DOI: 10.18653/v1/2020.findings-emnlp.4.

[23] D. Patel, S. Shah, and H. Chhinkaniwala, "Fuzzy logic based multi document summarization with improved sentence scoring and redundancy removal technique", *Expert Systems with Applications*, vol. 134, pp. 167–177, 2019. DOI: 10.1016/j.eswa.2019.05.045.

[24] P. Verma and H. Om, "MCRMR: Maximum coverage and relevancy with minimal redundancy based multi-document summarization", *Expert Systems with Applications*, vol. 120, pp. 43–56, 2019. DOI: 10.1016/j.eswa.2018.11.022.

[25] K. Lu, P. Mardziel, F. Wu, P. Amancharla, and A. Datta, "Gender bias in neural natural language processing", in *Logic, Language, and Security: Essays Dedicated to Andre Scedrov on the Occasion of His 65th Birthday*. Springer International Publishing, 2020, pp. 189–202. DOI: 10.1007/978-3-030-62077-6_14.

[26] T. Spinde *et al.*, "Automated identification of bias inducing words in news articles using linguistic and context-oriented features", *Information Processing & Management*, vol. 58, no. 3, 2021. DOI: 10.1016/j.ipm.2021.102505.

[27] C. van der Lee, E. Krahmer, and S. Wubben, "Automated learning of templates for data-to-text generation: Comparing rule-based, statistical and neural methods", in *Proceedings of the 11th International Conference on Natural Language Generation*, Tilburg University, The Netherlands: Association for Computational Linguistics, 2018, pp. 35–45. DOI: 10.18653/v1/W18-6504.

[28] J. Sun, Y. Wang, and Z. Li, "An improved template representation-based transformer for abstractive text summarization", in *2020 International Joint Conference on Neural Networks (IJCNN)*, IEEE, 2020. DOI: 10.1109/ijcnn48605.2020.9207609.

[29] I. M. Bilal *et al.*, "Template-based abstractive microblog opinion summarization", *Transactions of the Association for Computational Linguistics*, vol. 10, pp. 1229–1248, 2022. DOI: 10.1162/tacl_a_00516.

[30] X. Liu, H. Huang, G. Shi, and B. Wang, "Dynamic prefix-tuning for generative template-based event extraction", in *Proceedings of the 60th Annual Meeting of the Association for Computational Linguistics (Volume 1: Long Papers)*, Association for Computational Linguistics, 2022, pp. 5216–5228. DOI: 10.18653/v1/2022.acl-long.358.

[31] I. Cachola, K. Lo, A. Cohan, and D. Weld, "TLDR: Extreme summarization of scientific documents", in *Findings of the Association for Computational Linguistics: EMNLP 2020*, Association for Computational Linguistics, 2020, pp. 4766–4777. DOI: 10.18653/v1/2020.findings-emnlp.428.

[32] B. Gliwa, I. Mochol, M. Biesek, and A. Wawer, "SAMSum corpus: A human-annotated dialogue dataset for abstractive summarization", in *Proceedings of the 2nd Workshop on New Frontiers in Summarization*, Association for Computational Linguistics, 2019, pp. 70–79. DOI: 10.18653/v1/d19-5409.

[33] J. Zhang, Y. Zhao, M. Saleh, and P. Liu, "PEGASUS: Pre-training with extracted gap-sentences for abstractive summarization", in *Proceedings of the 37th International Conference on Machine Learning*, H. D. III and A. Singh, Eds., ser. Proceedings of Machine Learning Research, vol. 119, PMLR, 2020, pp. 11 328–11 339.

[34] M. Guo *et al.*, "LongT5: Efficient text-to-text transformer for long sequences", in *Findings of the Association for Computational Linguistics: NAACL 2022*, Association for Computational Linguistics, 2022, pp. 724–736. DOI: 10.18653/v1/2022.findings-naacl.55.

[35] R. Flesch, "A new readability yardstick.", *Journal of applied psychology*, vol. 32, no. 3, p. 221, 1948.

[36] G. Thomas, R. D. Hartley, and J. P. Kincaid, "Test-retest and inter-analyst reliability of the automated readability index, flesch reading ease score, and the fog count", *Journal of Reading Behavior*, vol. 7, no. 2, pp. 149–154, 1975.

[37] D. Fujs, S. Vrhovec, and D. Vavpotič, "Bibliometric mapping of research on user training for secure use of information systems", *JUCS - Journal of Universal Computer Science*, vol. 26, no. 7, pp. 764–782, 2020, ISSN: 0948-695X. DOI: 10.3897/jucs.2020.042. eprint: https://doi.org/10.3897/jucs.2020.042.

[38] S. Wendzel *et al.*, "Information security methodology, replication studies and information security education", *JUCS - Journal of Universal Computer Science*, vol. 26, no. 7, pp. 762–763, 2020, ISSN: 0948-695X. DOI: 10.3897/jucs.2020.041. eprint: https://doi.org/10.3897/jucs.2020.041.

Towards AI-Generated African Textile Patterns with StyleGAN and Stable Diffusion

Christelle Scharff, Samyak Rakesh Meshram, Krishna Mohan Bathula, FNU Kaleemunnisa, Om Gaikhe
Department of Computer Science
Pace University
New York, USA
e-mail: {cscharff, smeshram, kbathula, klnu, ogaikhe}@pace.edu

***Abstract*—Wax are traditional colorful textiles worn across Africa. They are composed of patterns of geometrical and symmetrical shapes that repeat indefinitely. This paper explores and compares the generation of African wax designs using StyleGan2-ADA, StyleGAN3 and Stable Diffusion architectures on a curated synthetic dataset of 2000 1024x1024 images obtained with DALL·E 2. The generated wax designs are evaluated using Fréchet Inception Distance (FID). StyleGAN2-ADA and Stable Diffusion generated better images. StyleGAN2-ADA generated designs diverse in colors, shapes and details with some symmetry and repetition. Stable Diffusion was stronger with symmetry and repetition, but it generated less details. By providing a new tool for creating customizable wax designs, this study has the potential to have an impact on the fashion industry. It is novel as it makes a case for inclusive AI by focusing on applications outside the scope of today's mainstream fashion industry. It also shows that the suggested approaches are promising to produce a variety of plausible and culturally appropriate designs. Our next step is to work with African fashion designers and wax experts to validate the resulting designs.**

Keywords-African wax patterns;* Fréchet Inception Distance (FID); *Stable Diffusion; StyleGAN.

I. Introduction

The fashion industry is one of the fastest growing sectors in Africa. African wax prints, also called Dutch wax prints, were introduced to Africa by Dutch merchants in the 19th century. Vlisco is the most widely known Dutch wax print textile manufacturer worldwide. Wax prints are widely present in West and Central Africa. They are bright colored cotton fabrics. The technique to create wax is inspired from the Indonesian hand-crafted batik method. The name "wax" comes from the technique based on heated wax and colored dyes to obtain the patterns on the fabrics. Wax print fabrics have recently reached a global audience and have been featured in fashion shows of international designers. Wax is recognized as a symbol of African identity worldwide. Wax designs are based on geometrical and special shapes and objects inspired from African culture and carrying meanings and messages. Patterns repeat indefinitely and are usually symmetrical. Some of the original and popular fabrics depict table fans to represent modernity, speed birds to symbolize volatile fortune, and alphabet to indicate literacy.

Creating African wax design is currently done using graphical editing software. Using Generative Artificial Intelligence (AI) would allow manufacturers to produce more designs in less time and guide the creative process with textual descriptions of different granularity of details.

This paper is a first attempt to generate wax designs using currently state-of-the-art generative AI techniques, StyleGAN [1][2] and stable diffusion [3]-[7] specifically. We curated a synthetic dataset of 2000 1024x1024 images generated with DALL·E 2. DALL·E is a general-purpose image generator. Our work focuses on wax generation, and it is expected that our generated wax will be better perceived than DALL·E by fashion professionals. Synthetic generated data are important to tackle problems when data are missing and to tap in new opportunities [8]. Our research relies on identifying the best performing models to generate representative wax designs. It is novel per the focus it takes on African fashion and the case it makes on inclusive AI focusing on applications outside the scope of today's mainstream fashion industry [9].

The paper is organized as follows. Section 2 provides background on StyleGAN and stable diffusion. Section 3 presents the dataset and the methodology we used. Section 4 covers the results we obtained. Section 5 concludes our work and outlines our future work.

II. Background

This section provides the context for this research, rooted in generative AI, and focuses on GAN and Stable Diffusion as generative AI models. It presents research initiatives on generative AI in fashion. It describes methods used to evaluate generated images, with an emphasis on Fréchet Inception Distance (FID).

A. GAN

Generative Adversarial Networks (GAN) [10] have gained popularity commercially in the last ten years, recently illustrated by the launch of the OpenAI DALL.E system that generates images from descriptive text. Part of unsupervised learning techniques, GAN aim at synthesizing huge amounts of images to create realistic new images. GAN reformulate the problem in terms of supervised learning where the generator produces new images and the discriminator classifies them as "real" or "fake".

B. GAN in Fashion

GAN have been highlighted in projects related to heritage, tradition, culture and art [11]-[15]. Fashion has generated numerous interesting problems in computer vision and machine learning, including in the use of GAN. Several fashion datasets have been created recently, including 3D datasets [16][17]. GarmentGAN [18] transfers target clothing items to reference body generating realistic images; it permits to see how clothes could fit bodies. Other studies have focused on generating new clothing on an individual using GAN [19].

C. SytleGAN

StyleGAN [1] is an alternative generator architecture for GAN. This architecture leads to an automatically learned, unsupervised separation of high-level attributes and random variation in the new generated images. It improves the state-of-the-art interpolation properties in terms of traditional measures of distribution quality. It permits to generate more photo-realistic high-quality images and to control the style of the generated images by focusing on different types of details. StyleGAN has been extended to StyleGAN2 [2] to reduce water-droplet artifacts appearing in StyleGAN images, StyleGAN2-ADA [5] to train GAN with limited amounts of data, and StyleGAN3 [20] to address image rotation and translation challenges.

D. Stable Diffusion and Latent Diffusion

Stable Diffusion and Latent Diffusion models, such as Stability AI SDXL 1.0 represent significant advancements in generative AI [4][6][21]. They operate by gradually transforming random noise into coherent images, leveraging a deep learning technique known as denoising. This process is guided by textual descriptions, allowing for the generation of detailed and contextually relevant elements. The latent diffusion approach further enhances this by operating in a latent space [22]. This latent space is a compressed representation of data, enabling more efficient and controllable image synthesis. The technique relies on a Variational Autoencoder (VAE) to map images to and from this latent space, and a Denoising Diffusion Probabilistic Model (DDPM) to iteratively refine these images [23]. This combination results in high-quality image generation with remarkable detail and coherence. The development of such models marks a significant improvement in creative AI.

E. Evaluating Generated Images

Evaluating generated images relies on quantitative and qualitative metrics. Inception Score (IS) is one of these metrics; it assesses images based on realism, clarity and diversity. While IS only evaluates the distribution of generated images, FID [24]-[26] compares the distribution of generated images with the distribution of a set of real images, indicating the model's performance in terms of replicating real-image statistics. It is used to evaluate generated images in terms of quality, diversity, and realism. Lowest scores for FID indicate more similarities between the generated and real images, signifying better quality. The approach that FID uses is to have the image embedded in a low-dimensional space using a state-of-the-art image recognition model, the one with the highest accuracy to measure the distribution distance in that space. For analyzing images, FID is typically based on the Inception-v3 mode [27] as it is well suited for GAN imagery. FID has several limitations including its unique application to images, its insensitivity to certain fine-grained details, its subjectivity that does not capture all aspects of human perception and preferences, and its requirements on the preprocessing of the images (scale, cropping and normalization). FID and other evaluation metrics should be coupled with Subject Matter Expert (SME) evaluation to judge the realism and details of generated images.

In addition to FID, Perceptual Path Length (PPL) was introduced as part of StyleGAN to evaluate generated images [2][28]. It measures the smoothness of transitions in the latent space, reflecting on the consistency and coherence of the image transformation. It also evaluates the diversity of generated images, ensuring the production of a wide range of distinct and plausible images, rather than the replication of a limited set of patterns. PPL [2][7], like FID, uses the feature embeddings of deep convolutional neural networks, but uses VGG16 network [29] instead of Inception-v3.

The assessment of FID scores in diffusion models like Stable Diffusion is markedly challenging [3]. FID scores measure the similarity between generated images and real images, based on features extracted by an Inception-v3 model, which is not used in Stable Diffusion. For Stable Diffusion models, the evaluation process is complex due to the time required to generate a sufficient number of images for accurate FID computation, StyleGAN models typically generate more images in the process. In addition to time constraints, the generation of this large number of images is also resource-intensive. Another aspect to consider is that the evaluation of Stable Diffusion models might also require investigating the model's ability to handle conditional image generation tasks, where the diffusion process is guided by textual descriptions or other forms of conditioning to produce images that are aligned with the given inputs. Lastly, researchers often explore the robustness and bias of the model, ensuring it generates diverse and fair outputs across various domains.

Qualitative evaluation is often necessary to complement quantitative metrics when evaluating generated images. It is based on human involvement to assess the realism and artistic quality of the outputs. The involvement of subject matter experts is crucial as some fine-grained elements related to the domain may not have been captured by the model.

III. METHODOLOGY

Our approach is based on experimenting with StyleGAN2-ADA, StyleGAN3 and Stable Diffusion on a curated synthetic dataset composed of wax pattern images.

A. Dataset

We curated a synthetic dataset (2K-Dataset) consisting of 2000 1024x1024 images collected from DALL·E 2. Per the Content Policy & Terms of DALL·E, we own the generated images. The reason for this synthetic dataset is that there is no dedicated wax dataset available. When evaluated qualitatively by fashion experts, DALL·E generated images have some similarities with wax but there is room for improvement. DALL·E is a general-purpose image generator. Our work focuses on wax generation, and it is expected that our generated wax will be better perceived by fashion professionals. These images were carefully selected to represent a diverse range of African wax designs, capturing different patterns, colors, and cultural motifs. To avoid biases in the images collected, such as color, design, pattern, and to ensure that the generated images are not duplicates, we used carefully selected predefined prompts (e.g., Green African wax', 'African wax textile pattern with traditional African symbols of Adire brown color', 'African wax textile pattern design inspired by modern styles with flowers in red'). Preprocessing steps, such as normalization, were applied to the 2K-Dataset to ensure optimal training performance. Figure 1 presents samples of our dataset.

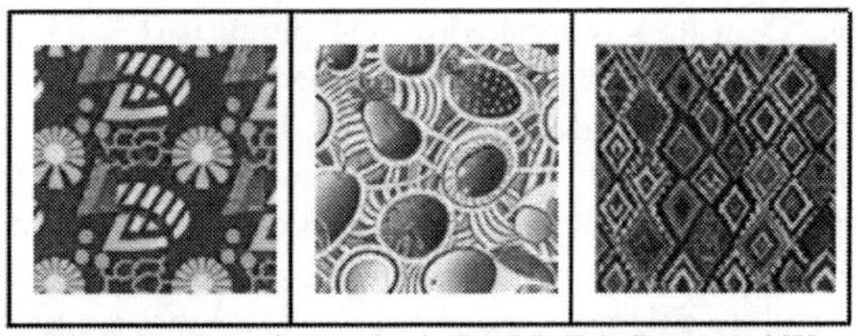

Figure 1. Sample Synthetic DALL·E 2 Generated Wax 1024x1024 Images Used in the 2K-Dataset.

B. Experimentation

We used StyleGAN2-ADA, StyleGAN3 and Stable Diffusion as architectures and experimented with the 2K-Dataset. The training was done on the university High Performance Computer (HPC) on two nodes. Each node is a 2x Intel(R) Xeon(R) Gold 6136 CPU @ 3.00GHz (24 cores total), 384GB RAM and 3x Nvidia Tesla V100 GPUs.

1) StyleGAN2-ADA and StyleGAN3

In StyleGAN2-ADA and StyleGAN3, we used mirroring to increase the dataset size and hyperparameters in the augmentation pipeline, such as blit, geometry, color, filter and noise, and applied factors, such as scaling, rotation, brightness and contrast. We saved intermediate results as snapshots to monitor model training without storing its weights. We assigned 2 to map_depth, 0.25 to the general learning rate, and 0.25 to the discriminator learning rate. We started by initializing the model's weights and optimized them to minimize the FID.

We reached 35.57 as the FID for StyleGAN2-ADA and 65.27 for StyleGAN3 as the lowest FID. Figures 2 and 3 show samples of wax designs generated for these FID. When training StyleGAN, "kimgs" (thousands of images) serves as a measure of how much experience the model has gained with a particular type of data. This exposure is crucial for the model to understand and capture the unique characteristics, colors, textures, and designs inherent in images, in our case African wax patterns. The more kimgs the model is trained with, the more refined and accurate its generated patterns tend to be. In our experiment, we went up to 5000 kimgs. In practice, experiments have shown that 5000 kimgs is a good benchmark to show strong performance on a variety of datasets. As a result, it has become a somewhat standard training unit. There is however a balance to consider as overtraining (exposing the model to too many images) can lead to overfitting, where the model performs well on the training data but poorly on new, unseen data. In the context of StyleGAN and African wax patterns, the goal is to train the model with enough kimgs to effectively capture the diversity and complexity of these patterns, enabling it to generate new, high-quality designs that are both novel and representative of the style. Figure 4 shows the evolution of the FID in StyleGAN2-ADA and StyleGAN3 with the learning progress of the models, showing that StyleGAN2-ADA permits to obtain a better FID and that a plateau is obtained after 4000 kimgs.

Figure 2. Generated patterns of African wax designs using StyleGAN2-ADA with 1024x1024 images (FID 35.57).

Figure 3. Generated patterns of African wax designs using StyleGAN3 with 1024x1024 images (FID 65.27).

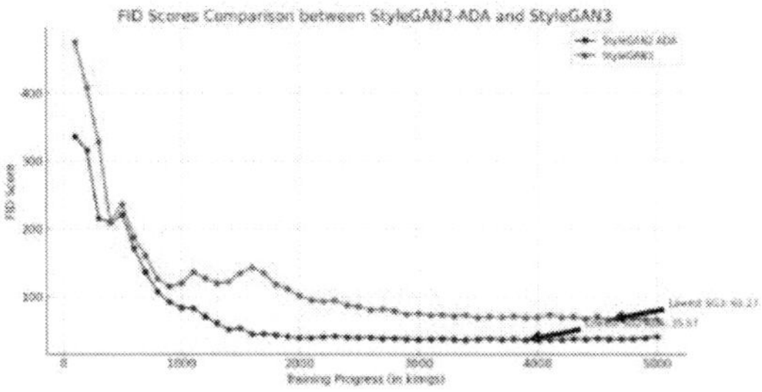

Figure 4. Training Progress of StyleGAN2-ADA and StyleGAN3 in Kimgs Depicting FID.

2) Stable Diffusion

The training of the Stable Diffusion model (Stability AI/SDXL 1.0) was conducted using the DreamBooth training method [30]. DreamBooth is an approach distinct from traditional GAN methods introducing unique training elements, such as personalized image generation, regularization techniques, and fine-tuning of pre-trained models. Unlike StyleGAN that focuses on generating diverse images from a large dataset, DreamBooth tailors the generation process to create images that are specific to a smaller, targeted dataset. It employs regularization techniques to maintain generalization abilities of the model while learning from a limited number of images. Instead of training the model from scratch like, it fine-tunes a pre-trained diffusion model on a small set of target images. Figure 5 presents resulting wax designs obtained with Stable Diffusion with FID of 226.75. In our approach, FID scores were calculated by generating 1000 images using our trained Diffusion Model, followed by comparing these images to our original dataset of 2000 images. This method, though resource-intensive, provided a feasible approach to gauge the model's performance.

Figure 5. Generated patterns of African wax designs using Stable Diffusion (FID 226.75) Prompt: Prompt: "Afwapa, beautiful african wax pattern with blue and black designs". Afwapa is a class name required by Dreambooth meaning AFrican WAx PAttern.

IV. Results

In the considered application of generating African wax designs, StyleGAN2-ADA, StyleGAN3, and the Stable Diffusion (Stability AI SDXL) models showcased varied performances and nuances in the production of the generated images. StyleGAN models are dedicated to learn and mimic complex distributions from training data. When trained on the 2K-Dataset of African wax patterns, StyleGAN2-ADA and StyleGAN3 models attempt to capture the high-level abstract features and the distribution of colors, shapes, and patterns that define the African wax style. Since they are GAN, the training process involves the generator trying to produce new images that the discriminator cannot distinguish from real African wax designs. The models do this by internalizing the nuances of the training images, ranging from geometric repetitions to the intricate designs typical of African wax prints. StyleGAN architectures were capable of capturing global and local patterns, which are important for the coherent generation of such designs. However, in general, the quality of the generated images can vary depending on factors, such as the diversity and size of the training dataset, the alignment of images, the model capacity, and the specifics of the training data.

In the case of Stable Diffusion models, when fine-tuned on African wax designs, the model leveraged the characteristics of these patterns more directly throughout the image generation process. This could result in a higher fidelity to the specific overall style of African wax patterns, especially if the fine-tuning process is meticulously guided to preserve the defining features of the prints.

The StyleGAN2-ADA model achieved the lowest FID score of 35.57, indicating a high similarity between the generated images and the training dataset. This suggests that StyleGAN2-ADA effectively captures the intricate designs and color patterns characteristic of African Wax Patterns, possibly due to its robust architecture and data compatibility. The StyleGAN3 model, with an FID score of 65.27, did not perform as well as StyleGAN2-ADA in this specific task. Possible reasons for this might include the fact that StyleGAN3 might not be as optimized and sensitive as StyleGAN2-ADA to specific smooth transitions, textures and patterns present in African wax designs. We also noticed that some colors appeared dominant in the StyleGAN3 generated images, such as green and orange. On the other hand, despite its higher FID score of 226.75, the Stable Diffusion model is better in symmetry, image quality, and granular control through text-to-image guidance. This suggests a different focus of the model, prioritizing creative control and qualitative aspects of image generation over strict adherence to the training dataset's statistical properties. Its higher FID score could be indicative of a trade-off between creative diversity and statistical accuracy.

While StyleGAN2-ADA shows a strong ability to accurately replicate the statistical properties of the training dataset for African Wax Patterns, the StyleGAN3 model's performance indicates a potential mismatch between its optimization objectives and the specific characteristics of the dataset. The Stable Diffusion model, despite a higher

FID score, offers significant advantages in terms of creative versatility and control, making it a valuable tool for tasks prioritizing these aspects. Based on our results, StyleGAN2-ADA generated African wax designs diverse in colors, shapes and details with some symmetry and repetition. Stable Diffusion was stronger with symmetry and repetition, but it generated less details. The choice among these models should be guided by the specific requirements of the task, whether it is the faithful reproduction of a dataset, creative image generation, or a balance between the two.

V. Conclusion and Future Work

This paper explored and compared the generation of African wax designs using StyleGan2-ADA, StyleGAN3 and Stable Diffusion architectures on a curated dataset of 2000 1024x1024 images generated with DALL·E 2. Our work is documented at [31].

StyleGAN2-ADA generated designs diverse in colors, shapes and details with some symmetry and repetition. Stable Diffusion was stronger with symmetry and repetition, but it generated less details. StyleGAN3 did not perform well on the dedicated task. The generated wax designs were evaluated using FID. While FID makes a lot of sense when used for StyleGAN, it is not the most adapted metrics for the nature of Stable Diffusion. We also evaluated the generated images qualitatively within the research team and based on our experience. DALL·E is a general-purpose image generation system; we focused on a very specific problem of wax pattern generation and obtained a higher level of details and, sometimes, symmetry. While we presented only a selection of the images, more images in the FID-range could have been provided to support our case. We plan to involve subject matter experts to refine the results, including by creating a significant synthetic dataset of African wax designs from the generated images to be used in the fashion sector. Fashion is a widely studied area of AI. This work has potential to impact fashion, one, by focusing on African fashion applications outside the scope of today's mainstream fashion industry, and, second, by providing designers with a new tool for creating customizable wax designs. In addition, we used a synthetic set of images obtained with DALL·E 2, but plan to work with wax print textile manufacturers on their wax patterns to compare the results.

References

[1] T. Karras, T., S. Laine and T. Aila. (2018). A Style-Based Generator Architecture for Generative Adversarial Networks. ArXiv. https://doi.org/10.48550/arXiv.1812.04948

[2] T. Karras et al., "Analyzing and Improving the Image Quality of StyleGAN," in 2020 IEEE/CVF Conference on Computer Vision and Pattern Recognition (CVPR), Seattle, WA, USA, 2020 pp. 8107-8116. doi: 10.1109/CVPR42600.2020.00813

[3] A. Borji. (2022). Generated faces in the wild: Quantitative comparison of stable diffusion, midjourney and dall-e 2. arXiv preprint arXiv:2210.00586.

[4] J. Ho, A. Jain and P. Abbeel. 2020. Denoising diffusion probabilistic models. In Proceedings of the 34th International Conference on Neural Information Processing Systems (NIPS'20). Curran Associates Inc., Red Hook, NY, USA, Article 574, 6840–6851.

[5] T. Karras, M. Aittala, S. Laine, E. Härkönen, J., Hellsten, J. Lehtinen and T. Aila. (2021). Alias-Free Generative Adversarial Networks. ArXiv. https://arxiv.org/abs/2106.12423

[6] J. Song, C. Meng and S. Ermon. (2020). Denoising diffusion implicit models. arXiv preprint arXiv:2010.02502.

[7] R. Zhang, P. Isola, A. A. Efros, E. Shechtman, E. and O. Wang. (2018). The Unreasonable Effectiveness of Deep Features as a Perceptual Metric. In Proceedings - 2018 IEEE/CVF Conference on Computer Vision and Pattern Recognition, CVPR 2018 (pp. 586-595). Article 8578166 (Proceedings of the IEEE Computer Society Conference on Computer Vision and Pattern Recognition). IEEE Computer Society. https://doi.org/10.1109/CVPR.2018.00068

[8] S. Aydore, Q., Zhaozhi and M. Van Der Schaar. Synthetic Data Generation with Generative AI. Workshop at NeurIPS 2023, December 2023.

[9] C. Scharff, J. Brusseau, K. M. Bathula, Kaleemunnisa, S. M. Meshram, O. Gaikhe. Inclusion Ethics in AI: Use Cases in African Fashion. AAAI-24 Spring Symposium on Increasing Diversity in AI Education and Research.

[10] I. J. Goodfellow, J. Pouget-Abadie, M. Mirza, B. Xu, D. Warde-Farley, S. Ozair, A. Courville and Y. Bengio. (2014). Generative Adversarial Networks. ArXiv. https://doi.org/10.48550/arXiv.1406.2661

[11] S. S Chen, H. Cui, P. Tan, X. Sun, X., Y. Ji and H. Duh. (2020). Cantonese porcelain image generation using user-guided generative adversarial networks. IEEE Computer Graphics and Applications, 40(5), 100–107. https://doi.org/10.1109/mcg.2020.3012079

[12] N. Matsumura, H. Tokura, Y. Kuroda, Y. Ito and K. Nakano. (2018). Tile art image generation using conditional generative adversarial networks. 2018 Sixth International Symposium on Computing and Networking Workshops (CANDARW). https://doi.org/10.1109/candarw.2018.00047

[13] S. S. Nasrin and R. I. Rasel. (2020). Hennagan: Henna art design generation using deep convolutional generative Adversarial Network (DCGAN). 2020 IEEE International Women in Engineering (WIE) Conference on Electrical and Computer Engineering (WIECON-ECE). https://doi.org/10.1109/wiecon-ece52138.2020.9398005

[14] S. Shahriar and K. Hayawi. (2022). NFTGAN: Non-fungible token art generation using generative adversarial networks. 2022 7th International Conference on Machine Learning Technologies (ICMLT). https://doi.org/10.1145/3529399.3529439

[15] Y. Yin, Z. Chen, Y. Zhao, J. Li and K. Zhang. (2020). Automated Chinese seal carving art creation with Ai Assistance. 2020 IEEE Conference on Multimedia Information Processing and Retrieval (MIPR). https://doi.org/10.1109/mipr49039.2020.00086

[16] H. Zhu. Y. Cao, H. Jin, W. Chen, D. Du, Z. Wang, S. Cui and X. Han. (2020). Deep Fashion3D: A Dataset and Benchmark for 3D Garment Reconstruction from Single Images. ArXiv. https://doi.org/10.48550/arXiv.2003.12753

[17] X. Zou, X. Kong, W. Wong, C. Wang, Y. Liu and Y. Cao. (2019). FashionAI: A Hierarchical Dataset for Fashion Understanding. IEEE/CVF Conference on Computer Vision and Pattern Recognition Workshops (CVPRW), Long Beach, CA, USA, 2019, pp. 296-304, doi: 10.1109/CVPRW.2019.00039.

[18] A. H. Raffiee and M. Sollami. (2020). GarmentGAN: Photo-realistic Adversarial Fashion Transfer. ArXiv. https://doi.org/10.48550/arXiv.2003.01894

[19] S. Zhu, S. Fidler, R. Urtasun, D. Lin and C. C. Loy. (2017). Be Your Own Prada: Fashion Synthesis with Structural Coherence. ArXiv. https://doi.org/10.48550/arXiv.1710.07346

[20] T. Karras, M. Aittala, J. Hellsten, S. Laine, J. Lehtinen and T. Aila. (2020). Training Generative Adversarial Networks with Limited Data. ArXiv. https://doi.org/10.48550/arXiv.2006.06676

[21] P. Dhariwal and A. Nichol. (2021). Diffusion models beat gans on image synthesis. Advances in neural information processing systems, 34, 8780-8794.

[22] R. Rombach, A. Blattmann, D. Lorenz, P. Esser and B. Ommer. (2022). High-resolution image synthesis with latent diffusion models. In Proceedings of the IEEE/CVF conference on computer vision and pattern recognition (pp. 10684-10695).

[23] D. P. Kingma and M. Welling. (2013). Auto-encoding variational bayes. arXiv preprint arXiv:1312.6114.

[24] M. Heusel, H. Ramsauer, T. Unterthiner, B. Nessler and S. Hochreiter. (2017). GANs Trained by a Two Time-Scale Update Rule Converge to a Local Nash Equilibrium. ArXiv. https://doi.org/10.48550/arXiv.1706.08500

[25] E. J. Nunn, P. Khadivi and S. Samavi. (2021). Compound Frechet Inception Distance for Quality Assessment of GAN Created Images. ArXiv. https://doi.org/10.48550/arXiv.2106.08575

[26] M. Soloveitchik, T. Diskin, E. Morin and A. Wiesel. (2021). Conditional Frechet Inception Distance. ArXiv. https://doi.org/10.48550/arXiv.2103.11521

[27] C. Szegedy et al. (2015) Going deeper with convolutions. In 2015 IEEE Conference on Computer Vision and Pattern Recognition (CVPR), Boston, MA, USA, 2015 pp. 1-9. doi: 10.1109/CVPR.2015.7298594

[28] J. Sohl-Dickstein, E. À. Weiss, N. Maheswaranathan and S. Ganguli. 2015. Deep unsupervised learning using nonequilibrium thermodynamics. In Proceedings of the 32nd International Conference on International Conference on Machine Learning - Volume 37 (ICML'15). JMLR.org, 2256–2265.

[29] K. Simonyan and A. Zisserman. (2014) Very Deep Convolutional Networks for Large-Scale Image Recognition. http://arxiv.org/abs/1409.1556

[30] N. Ruiz, Y. Li, V., Jampani, Y. Pritch, M. Rubinstein and K. Aberman. (2023). Dreambooth: Fine tuning text-to-image diffusion models for subject-driven generation. In Proceedings of the IEEE/CVF Conference on Computer Vision and Pattern Recognition (pp. 22500-22510).

[31] Scharff, C., Meshram, S. R., Bathula, K. M., Kaleemunnisa and Gaikhe, O. https://github.com/researchpace/waxfashion.

Fuzzy Agent-Based Simulation of Integrated Solutions for Task Allocation and Battery Charge Management for Fleets of Autonomous Industrial Vehicles

Juliette Grosset
ECAM Rennes – Louis de Broglie
IMT Atlantique – IRISA, UMR 6074
Rennes, France
Email : juliette.grosset@ecam-rennes.fr

Alain-Jérôme Fougères
ECAM Rennes – Louis de Broglie
IT and Telecommunications Laboratory
Rennes, France
Email : alain-jerome.fougeres@ecam-rennes.fr

Moïse Djoko-Kouam
ECAM Rennes – Louis de Broglie
IETR, UMR CNRS 6164
Rennes, France
Email : moise.djoko-kouam@ecam-rennes.fr

Jean-Marie Bonnin
IMT Atlantique
IRISA, UMR 6074
Rennes, France
Email: jm.bonnin@imt-atlantique.fr

***Abstract*— The paper presents a multi-agent simulation using fuzzy inference to explore in an integrated way the task allocation and battery charging management of mobile baggage conveyor robots in an airport. This simulation approach offers high adaptability thanks to a distributed system, adapting to variations in the availability of conveyor agents, their battery capacity, knowledge of the context of infrastructure resource availability, and awareness of the activity of the conveyor fleet. Dynamic factors, such as workload variations and communication between the conveyor agents and infrastructure are considered as heuristics, highlighting the importance of flexible and collaborative approaches in autonomous systems. The results highlight the effectiveness of adaptive fuzzy multi-agent models to optimize dynamic task allocation, adapt to the variation of baggage arrival flows, improve the overall operational efficiency of conveyor agents, and reduce their energy consumption.**

Keywords-autonomous industrial vehicle; dynamique task allocation; fuzzy agent; agent-based simulation; Airport 4.0.

I. INTRODUCTION

The deployment of Autonomous Industrial Vehicle (AIV) fleets in the context of Airport 4.0 raises several issues, all related to their real level of autonomy: acceptance by employees, vehicle localization, traffic flow, failure detection, collision avoidance and vehicle perception in changing environments. Simulation makes it possible to take into account the various constraints and requirements formulated by manufacturers and future users of these AIVs.

Before starting to test AIV fleet traffic scenarios in often-complex airport situations, it is wise, if not essential, to simulate these scenarios [1]. Moreover, one of the main advantages of using simulations is that the results can be used without the need to apply a scaling factor.

The main advantages of simulating mobile robot or AIV operations are: reducing the time and cost of developing an AIV, minimizing potential operational risks associated with AIVs, allowing to assess the feasibility of different AIV circulation scenarios at a strategic or operational level, allowing a rapid understanding of the operations carried out by AIVs, and identifying improvements in the layout configurations of the facilities hosting these AIVs [2].

Simulation also provides flexibility in terms of AIV deployment and allows studying the sharing of responsibility between the central server and the robots (local/global or centralized/decentralized balance) for the different operational decisions. Another advantage of simulations is to introduce humans into the scenarios in order to verify and validate, before the actual deployment of autonomous mobile robots, the safety of the coexistence and possible interactions between these AIVs and human operators [3]. Agent-based approaches are often proposed for the simulation of autonomous vehicles. They offer simulation contexts ranging from trajectory planning to optimal task allocation, while allowing collision and obstacle avoidance [4].

Our current research focuses on the use of fuzzy agents to handle the levels of imprecision and uncertainty involved in modeling the behavior of simulated vehicles [5]. Indeed, fuzzy set theory is well suited to the processing of uncertain or imprecise information that must lead to decision-making by autonomous agents, used in activities such as the simulation of AIVs in an airport or product design [6].

Fuzzy agents can track the evolution of fuzzy information from their environment and from agents [7]. By interpreting the fuzzy information they receive or perceive, fuzzy agents interact within the multi-agent system of which they are a part. For example, a fuzzy agent can discriminate a fuzzy interaction value to assess its degree of affinity (or interest) with another fuzzy agent [8].

Thus, we develop a comprehensive study on utilizing fuzzy inference within multi-agent simulations to optimize task allocation and battery management for mobile baggage conveyor robots in airports. The proposed simulation approach is designed to be highly adaptable, taking into account dynamic factors such as workload variations, battery capacities, and communication between agents and infrastructure. The results demonstrate that this adaptive fuzzy multi-agent model can significantly improve operational efficiency, adapt to variations in baggage arrival flows, and reduce energy consumption.

This article is structured as follows: first, we present a state-of-the art on the fuzzy agent-based allocation of tasks; then, we propose a case study on fuzzy task allocation where we compare five kinds of strategies; in Section 4 we present three improvements using fuzzy heuristics; finally, we conclude on the proposed fuzzy dynamic task allocation strategies, and then we present different work perspectives.

II. FUZZY AGENT-BASED TASK ALLOCATION

This section presents a brief state of the art on task allocation and fuzzy agent-based simulation.

A. *Task allocation*

Task Allocation (TA) consists of optimally assigning a set of tasks to be performed by agents, actors, robots or processes, grouped and organized within a cohesive system. This is the case for mobile multi-robot systems [9], AIV fleets [10], and applications in airports [11].

In the field of mobile robotics, the taxonomy presented in [12] has been defined to better characterize allocation and assignment functions to robots: Single Task for a Single Robot (STSR), Multiple Tasks for a Single Robot (MTSR), and Multiple Tasks for Multiple Robots (MTMR). These classifications enable tasks to be assigned to one or multiple robots, with various tasks being allocated to heterogeneous or multitasking robots.

Moreover, De Ryck et al. [12] defined also: allocation modalities, such as instantaneous allocation or allocation extended in time. This last is linked to synchronization and precedent or time window constraints. As many combinations as exhaustively detailed by numerous surveys on the issue of multi-robot TA.

Different solution models have been proposed for TA: based on optimization: exact algorithms, dynamic programming, (meta-)heuristics [9]; based on the Contract Net Protocol: inside an agent-based system, an initiating agent sends a call for proposals to all agents, chooses the best proposal received, and then informs all agents [10]; based on the concept of the market: announcement by an auctioneer, submission by bidders, selection by the auctioneer and award by the auctioneer [13].

Furthermore, different types of optimization objectives can be defined for this task allocation [12]: cost objectives (travel costs, such as time, distance or fuel consumption), behavior objectives (ability of a robot to perform a task), reward objectives (payoff for performing a task), priority objectives (urgency to perform a task), and utility objectives (subtracting the cost from the reward or fitness).

Task allocation and planning are often managed centrally, even semi-centrally when global and local planning are differentiated [14]. For the proper functioning of autonomous and dynamic systems, the requirements of flexibility, robustness and scalability, lead to consider decentralized mechanisms to react to unexpected situations. Autonomy and decentralization are two excessively linked notions to the extent that an autonomous system operates and makes decisions autonomously [15]. The problem of task allocation can also be thought of in a decentralized way [12].

For reasons of flexibility, robustness and scalability necessary in an Industry 4.0 or Airport 4.0 context, we are interested in decentralized task allocation solutions. These solutions, decomposed below, must be able to assign tasks to a fleet of robots.

Particularly, solutions based on the market concept can easily be applied in a distributed context, where each mobile robot can become an auctioneer [16]. For each situation, a single mobile robot is appointed auctioneer, and retains this role until the situation is definitively managed

B. *Fuzzy agent-based simulation*

Many agent-based approaches are proposed for the simulation of autonomous vehicles. They offer simulation contexts ranging from trajectory planning [17] to optimal task allocation, while allowing collision and obstacle avoidance [18]. Our current research focuses on the use of fuzzy agents to handle the levels of imprecision and uncertainty involved in modeling the behavior of simulated vehicles [5]. Fuzzy set theory is well suited to the processing of uncertain or imprecise information that must lead to decision-making by autonomous agents [6].

Most of the control tasks performed by autonomous mobile robots have been the subject of performance improvement studies using fuzzy logic [19]: navigation [20], obstacle avoidance [21], path planning [22], motion planning [23], localization of mobile robots [24], and intelligent management of energy consumption [25].

An agent-based system is fuzzy if its agents have fuzzy behaviors or if the knowledge they use is fuzzy [26]. This means that agents can have: 1) fuzzy knowledge (fuzzy decision rules, fuzzy linguistic variables, and fuzzy linguistic values); 2) fuzzy behaviors (the behaviors adopted by agents because of fuzzy inferences); and 3) fuzzy interactions, organizations, or roles. The six equations below propose a model of fuzzy agents corresponding to the principles stated above and used in the simulations presented in this paper:

$$\tilde{M}_a = < \tilde{A}, \tilde{I}, \tilde{P}, \tilde{O} > \ . \tag{1}$$

Where $\tilde{A}$ is a set of fuzzy agents; $\tilde{I}$ is a set of fuzzy interactions between fuzzy agents; $\tilde{P}$ is a set of fuzzy roles that fuzzy agents can perform; and $\tilde{O}$ is a set of fuzzy organizations defined for fuzzy agents (subsets of strongly linked fuzzy agents).

$$\tilde{\alpha}_i = \left\langle \Phi_{\Pi(\tilde{\alpha}_i)}, \Phi_{\Delta(\tilde{\alpha}_i)}, \Phi_{\Gamma(\tilde{\alpha}_i)}, K_{\tilde{\alpha}_i} \right\rangle . \tag{2}$$

Where $\Phi_{\Pi(\tilde{\alpha}_i)}$ is the $\tilde{\alpha}_i$ function of observation; $\Phi_{\Delta(\tilde{\alpha}_i)}$ is the $\tilde{\alpha}_i$ function of decision; $\Phi_{\Gamma(\tilde{\alpha}_i)}$ is the $\tilde{\alpha}_i$ function of action; and $K_{\tilde{\alpha}_i}$ is the knowledge of the fuzzy agent $\tilde{\alpha}_i$.

$$\Phi_{\Pi(\tilde{\alpha}_i)} : (E_{\tilde{\alpha}_i} \cup I_{\tilde{\alpha}_i}) \times \Sigma_{\tilde{\alpha}_i} \rightarrow \Pi_{\tilde{\alpha}_i} \ . \tag{3}$$

$$\Phi_{\Delta(\tilde{\alpha}_i)} : \Pi_{\tilde{\alpha}_i} \times \Sigma_{\tilde{\alpha}_i} \rightarrow \Delta_{\tilde{\alpha}_i} . \quad (4)$$

$$\Phi_{\Gamma(\tilde{\alpha}_i)} : \Delta_{\tilde{\alpha}_i} \times \Sigma \rightarrow \Gamma_{\tilde{\alpha}_i} . \quad (5)$$

Where $E_{\tilde{\alpha}_i}$ is the $\tilde{\alpha}_i$ set of fuzzy observed events; $I_{\tilde{\alpha}_i}$ is the $\tilde{\alpha}_i$ set of fuzzy interactions; $\Sigma_{\tilde{\alpha}_i}$ is the $\tilde{\alpha}_i$ set of fuzzy state; $\Pi_{\tilde{\alpha}_i}$ is the $\tilde{\alpha}_i$ set of fuzzy perceptions; $\Delta_{\tilde{\alpha}_i}$ is the $\tilde{\alpha}_i$ set of fuzzy decisions; and $\Gamma_{\tilde{\alpha}_i}$ is the $\tilde{\alpha}_i$ set of fuzzy actions; Σ is the state of the fuzzy agent-based system $\tilde{M}_{\alpha}$.

$$\tilde{\iota}_i = < \tilde{\alpha}_s, \tilde{\alpha}_r, \tilde{\gamma}_c > . \quad (6)$$

Where $\tilde{\iota}_i$ is a fuzzy interaction; $\tilde{\alpha}_s$ is the fuzzy agent source of a fuzzy interaction; $\tilde{\alpha}_r$ is the fuzzy agent receiver of a fuzzy interaction; and $\tilde{\gamma}_c$ is a fuzzy communication act.

III. CASE STUDY: FUZZY TASK ALLOCATION SIMULATION

This case study proposes the simulation of mobile robots conveying baggage fleet in an airport (we will keep the name "AIV" for these conveyors). Figure 1 shows the simulator's HMI, which allows on the one hand, to visualize the arrival of baggage and the movements of 5 AIVs, and on the other hand, to follow the evolution of the different levels of indicators of the simulation (energy level, baggage level, charge level, and time level).

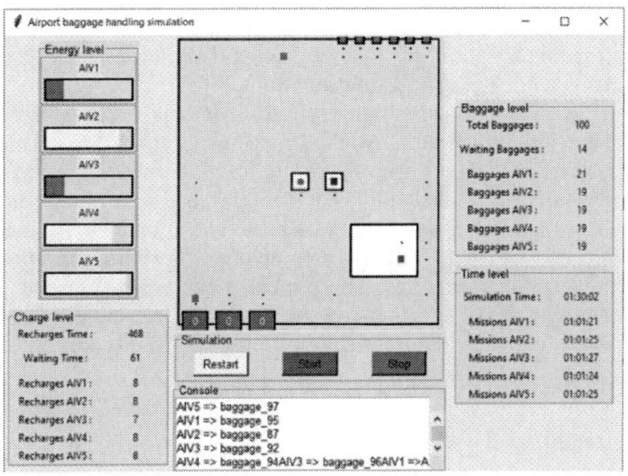

Figure 1. Simulation Application

Effective management of these AIVs requires an integrative approach that considers several factors, including the baggage arrival flow, the operational availability of the AIVs, their energy consumption, their communication, among themselves and with the infrastructure, and their adaptation to changing environmental conditions. In the case study, we analyze the TA performed by a supervisor who questions AIVs to know their task completion costs. Through 8 scenarios, we will progressively introduce fuzzy inferences to determine the costs of task completion, battery recharging and speed adjustment.

A. *The simulation framework*

Figure 2 presents the agent model proposed to test our dynamic task allocation strategies for AIVs in simulation. The objective is to have an agent-based modeling and simulation system designed generically to test different scenarios, but also different types of circulation plans.

An infrastructure is deployed in the environment. It is composed of a circulation plan and active elements, such as beacons, tags, the two charging stations and the two types of treadmill for baggage entry and exit. Static or dynamic obstacles (e.g., operators) may be present in the environment.

AIV fuzzy agents perform missions defined by paths on the traffic plan. AIV fuzzy agents are equipped with a radar to avoid collisions and have knowledge about the environment and other agents to operate and cooperate. AIV fuzzy agents communicate with each other with different types of standardized messages. AIV fuzzy agents have fuzzy and uncertain knowledge, but also incomplete and fragmented, in order to adapt to situations that are themselves uncertain. Baggage are objects managed by the environment: arrival flow on the entry treadmill, tracking of its localization, and exit from the circuit on the exit treadmill.

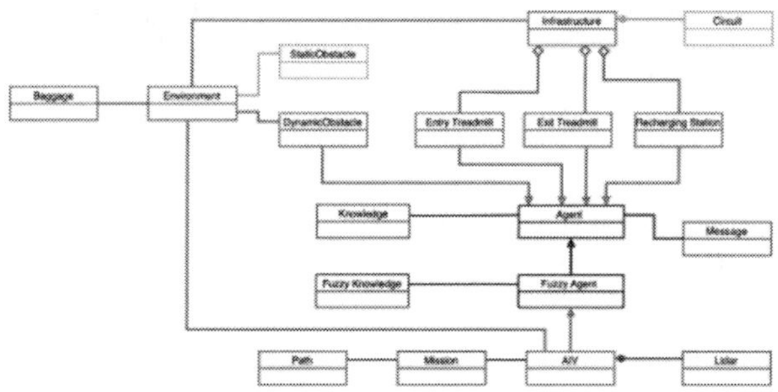

Figure 2. Simulator architecture: dynamic elements in red, static in green, and not related to the environment in purple.

B. *Task allocation with basic strategies*

In this section, we provide a comparative analysis of three basic types of auction-based task allocation strategies: random TA, FIFO TA, and AIV availability-based TA. Each of these strategies is tested in a scenario:

- *Sc1* (Random) is a TA scenario where missions are assigned to the AIV agents only randomly.
- *Sc2* (FIFO) is a TA scenario where missions are assigned to AIV agents using a queuing mechanism.
- *Sc3* (Available) is a TA scenario where missions are assigned to the most available AIV agents.

We simulated these three scenarios for 100 bags. We seek to minimize the maximum number of pending bags at a given time, the total simulation time, the average time to complete a mission per AIV agent, the number of missions completed per AIV agent during the simulation, and the activity rate per AIV agent. The simulation results are presented in Table 1.

Random strategy: the maximum number of pending bags is high, the simulation time is also high, and the allocation of missions and the activity rates of AIV agents are poorly balanced (the average activity rate at 0.72 is low). The random strategy does not allow allocation to AIV agents that are a priori available, which very quickly leads to pending bags to be processed and therefore poor results.

FIFO strategy: this strategy brings a clear improvement in the results. The maximum number of pending bags is very low, the simulation time is very correct, the allocation is almost uniform (only the stops for recharging the batteries cause imbalances), and the occupancy rate of the AIV agents is much better (0.84).

Available strategy: this strategy produces the best results, except for the maximum number of pending bags. Allocating a mission to an AIV agent that is more available than the others are therefore improves the results. However, it is necessary to better manage the allocation based on pending bags and energy consumption to consolidate (or even optimize) this strategy.

TABLE I. TASK ALLOCATION SIMULATION RESULTS IN SCENARIOS SC1, SC2 AND SC3, FOR 100 BAGS.

Scenarios	Random	FIFO	Available
Maximum nb of pending bags	19	4	8
Simulation time	2270s	1942s	1846s
Average mission time per AIV (in s)	[81,81,83,83,81]	[80,82,83,81,83]	[81,80,81,83,81]
Nb of missions completed by AIV	[26,26,14,14,20]	[21,21,19,21,18]	[22,21,20,19,18]
Work rate per AIV	[0.93,0.93,0.51, 0.51, 0.71]	[0.87, 0.89, 0.81, 0.88, 0.77]	[0.97, 0.91, 0.88, 0.85, 0.79]

C. *Task allocation with fuzzy strategies*

In this section, we propose an analysis of task allocation by auction based on a fuzzy inference approach. As a reminder, fuzzy logic allows us to better understand natural, uncertain, imprecise and difficult to model phenomena by relying on the definition of *if-then fuzzy* rules and membership functions (linguistic variables) to *fuzzy sets* [27].

Two scenarios are studied. The first, *Sc4*, implements a TA strategy in which each AIV agent uses a fuzzy model with 3 linguistic input variables (availability of the AIV agent, distance from the baggage drop-off location, energy level of the AIV agent) to determine the cost of handling a mission (picking up and dropping off a baggage). The second, *Sc5*, takes the strategy of *Sc4* and adds energy management with a second fuzzy model. With this new fuzzy model, the AIV agents determine whether they will need to recharge during a mission, which allows them to refine calculation of the mission cost. The linguistic variables used in this scenario are: availability of the AIV agent, distance from the baggage drop-off location, energy level of AIV agent, and distances of the 2 charging stations.

Fuzzy strategy in *Sc4*. The results with this new strategy are generally good: low maximum number of pending bags, good overall simulation time, good distribution of missions between AIV agents and good average AIV activity rate (0.88). However, few elements of uncertainty are considered (3 linguistic variables at the input and one at the output). The introduction of other fuzzy elements (nuances in the simulation parameters) should improve the results, particularly in terms of maximum number of pending bags and management of battery recharges.

Fuzzy strategies in *Sc5*. In this new scenario, the raw results of the TA are slightly worse than in *Sc4*: same maximum number of pending bags, slightly longer overall simulation time, worse distribution of missions between AIV agents and worse average AIV occupancy rate (0.82). However, the overall recharge time is lower in this scenario, which can allow a greater availability of AIV agents (an area of improvement for the next scenarios).

TABLE II. TASK ALLOCATION SIMULATION RESULTS IN SCENARIOS SC4 AND SC5, FOR 100 BAGS

Scenarios	Sc4	Sc5
Maximum nb of pending bags	6	6
Simulation time	1843s	2000s
Average mission time per AIV (in s)	[80, 81, 80, 81, 82]	[81, 80, 81, 84, 83]
Nb of missions completed by AIV	[21, 21, 21, 19, 18]	[23, 19, 21, 19, 18]
Work rate per AIV	[0.91,0.92,0.91,0.84,0.80]	[0.93,0.76,0.85,0.80,0.75]

TABLE III. RECHARGE SIMULATION RESULTS IN SCENARIOS SC4 AND SC5, FOR 100 BAGS

Scenarios	Sc4	Sc5
Recharge time	546s	490s
Waiting time for recharges	34s	16s
Nb of recharges	39	33
Distribution of nb of recharges per AIV	[8, 8, 8, 8, 7]	[8, 6, 7, 6, 6]

IV. IMPROVEMENT USING FUZZY HEURISTICS

Now, we propose to increase the relevance of previous auction TA scenarios based on a fuzzy inference approach, by integrating other types of realistic constraints concerning battery recharging and AIV agent speed adjustment made possible by a stronger knowledge of the fleet traffic and mission management context (increased awareness). Three scenarios are studied (*Sc6*, *Sc7* and *Sc8*) to show that specific heuristics allow us to treat certain situations quite finely and to increase the collective/global performances of the AIV agents. The results are presented in Table 4 for task allocation and Table 5 for battery recharging.

Sc6 consists of completing scenario *Sc5* to determine in which station the AIV agents can recharge in order to minimize the waiting times for recharging, based on knowledge of the context of occupation of the stations and the needs of the other AIV agents (therefore more awareness for the agents). The linguistic variables used in this sixth scenario are the following: the availability of the AIV agent, the distance from the baggage drop-off location, the energy level of the AIV agent, the distances of the 2 recharging stations and the availability of the recharging stations.

Sc7 takes up the strategy of *Sc6* and adapts the recharging rate (80 or 100%) in order to increase their availability if the flow of incoming baggage increases and therefore if the number of pending bags is likely to increase. The linguistic variables used in this seventh scenario are: the availability of the AIV agent, the distance from the baggage drop-off location, the energy level of the AIV agent, the distances from the 2 charging stations, the availability of the charging stations and a variable energy charge rate.

Sc8 consists of increasing *Sc7* by adapting/regulating the speed of the AIV agents according to the flow of baggage arrivals and therefore the potential increase in the number of pending bags to be processed, but also according to the speed, the proximity of other AIV agents (use of observed and safety distances). The linguistic variables used in this eighth scenario are as follows: the availability of the AIV agent, the distance from the baggage drop-off location, the energy level of the AIV agent, the distances of the 2 charging stations, the availability of the charging stations, a variable charging rate (80 or 100%) and urgency in relation to the number of pending bags.

Results of fuzzy inferences in *Sc6*. This is the implementation of a first heuristic to improve the TA but also the recharge decision. The objective is to minimize the waiting time for a recharge when an AIV agent must be available to take baggage. The results for TA are slightly better than in *Sc5*: the same maximum number of pending bags, a slightly shorter overall simulation time, a rather homogeneous average mission completion time, a better distribution of missions between AIV agents, and an average AIV activity rate that is roughly the same (0.82). However, if the overall recharge time is the same, the waiting time for recharges is significantly lower (14s).

Results of fuzzy inferences in *Sc7*. Second heuristic proposed in order to increase the availability of AIV agents so that they can take baggage according to their arrival flow while minimizing the waiting time for their recharges. In this scenario, the results for TA are significantly better than in the *Sc6* scenario: the same maximum number of pending bags, but a shorter overall simulation time, a more homogeneous average mission completion time, a better distribution of missions between AIV agents and a higher average AIV activity rate (0.84). Regarding battery recharges, the results are of the same order for both scenarios: an identical overall recharge time, with in *Sc7*, a slightly higher waiting time for recharges (18s).

Results of fuzzy inferences in *Sc8*. A third heuristic was proposed in order to adjust speed of the AIV agents to minimize the maximum number of pending bags when the flow of baggage arrivals increases. The results for TA are much better than in *Sc7*: the same maximum number of pending bags, but a much lower overall simulation time (a consequence of the adaptation of speeds of AIV agents when necessary), an average time of completion of the missions and a distribution of the missions between the AIV agents always homogeneous, and finally, a lower average occupancy rate of the AIV agents (0.79), because the last two AIV agents are less requested due to the adaptation of the speeds of the first 3, in particular their increase in speed to respond to the increase in the flow of baggage arrivals. As for the battery recharges, the results are less good: the increase in the speeds of the AIV agents has an energy cost!

TABLE IV. TASK ALLOCATION SIMULATION RESULTS IN SCENARIOS SC6; SC7 AND SC8, FOR 100 BAGS

Scenarios	Sc6	Sc7	Sc8
Maximum nb of pending bags	6	6	6
Simulation time	1964s	1896s	1675s
Average mission time per AIV (in s)	[79,79,80,80,81]	[79,80,80,80,80]	[67,65,67,65,67]
Nb of missions completed by AIV	[22,22,20,16,20]	[22,22,21,18,17]	[22,22,22,19,15]
Work rate per AIV	[0.88, 0.88, 0.81, 0.65, 0.82]	[0.92, 0.93, 0.89, 0.76, 0.72]	[0.88, 0.85, 0.88, 0.74, 0.6]

TABLE V. RECHARGE SIMULATION RESULTS IN SCENARIOS SC6, SC7 AND SC8, FOR 100 BAGS

Scenarios	Sc6	Sc7	Sc8
Recharge time	490	490	736
Wait time for recharges	14	18	119
Nb of recharges	33	33	49
Distribution of nb of recharges per AIV	[7, 7, 7, 5, 7]	[7, 7, 7, 6, 6]	[11, 11, 11, 9, 7]

V. CONCLUSION

We developed a multi-agent simulation platform to test different scenarios of task allocation management for mobile baggage conveyor robots (AIVs) in the context of Airport 4.0. This approach offers a flexible adaptation to the different aspects of AIV autonomy management and facilitates possible adjustments needed for deployment at an airport site. The use of a distributed multi-agent system provides temporary autonomy in case of central infrastructure failure, and can improve the management of individual AIV functions, such as task allocation, battery charging, speed regulation, etc.

To establish a basis for comparison of auction-based task allocation strategies with the fuzzy approach we wanted to develop, we started by defining three basic scenarios implementing random, FIFO and AIV availability strategies. We then tested a task allocation scenario with a basic fuzzy model, and then we made several improvements to this scenario by extending the AIV's fuzzy decision model to: (1) recharging the AIVs batteries, (2) determining the recharging station, (3) determining the most relevant recharging rate, and (4) regulating the speed of the AIVs so that they adapt to the variation of the baggage arrival flow.

The simulation results show that integrating adaptive fuzzy multi-agent models for managing task allocation, energy recharging management, determining the most favorable infrastructure elements (charging stations) and speed adaptation, can improve the operational efficiency of AIV fleet. These results highlight the importance of flexible and collaborative approaches to improve the performance of autonomous systems in dynamic environments.

We plan to continue integrating fuzzy models into AIV agent behavior simulations and to add learning capabilities (e.g., based on neural networks [28]) to them in order to increase the relevance and efficiency of their decisions in the collective management of their autonomies.

ACKNOWLEDGMENT

The authors would like to thank the Brittany region for funding the *VIASIC* and *ALPHA* projects, as part respectively of the ARED-2021-2024 call for projects, and the PME 2022 call for projects entitled "Accelerate time to market of digital technological innovations from SMEs in the Greater West".

REFERENCES

[1] X. Hu and B. P. Zeigler, "A Simulation-based Virtual Environment to Study Cooperative Robotic Systems," Integrated Computer-Aided Engineering, Vol. 12, Issue 4, 2005, pp. 353-367.

[2] N. Tsolakis, D. Bechtsis, J. S. Srai, "Intelligent autonomous vehicles in digital supply chains: From conceptualisation, to simulation modelling, to real-world operations," Business Process Management J., Vol. 25, Issue 3, 2019, pp. 414-437.

[3] A. Hentout, M. Aouache, A. Maoudj, I. Akli, "Human–robot interaction in industrial collaborative robotics: a literature review of the decade 2008–2017," Advanced Robotics, Vol. 33, Issue 15–16, 2019, pp. 764–799.

[4] P. Jing, H. Hu, F. Zhan, Y. Chen, Y. Shi, "Agent-based simulation of autonomous vehicles: A systematic literature review," IEEE Access, Vol. 8, 2020, pp. 79089-79103.

[5] A.-J. Fougères, "A Modelling Approach Based on Fuzzy Agent," Int. J. of Computer Science Issues, Vol. 9, Issue 6, 2013, pp. 19-28.

[6] A.-J. Fougères and E. Ostrosi, "Fuzzy agent-based approach for consensual design synthesis in product configuration," Integrated Computer-Aided Engineering, Vol. 20, Issue 3, 2013, pp. 259-274.

[7] N. Ghasem-Aghaee and T. I. Ören, "Towards Fuzzy Agents with Dynamic Personality for Human Behavior Simulation," Proc. of SCSC 2003, Montreal, Canada, 2003, pp. 3–10.

[8] E. Ostrosi, A.-J. Fougères, M. Ferney, "A fuzzy configuration multi-agent approach for product family modelling in conceptual design," Journal of Intelligent Manufacturing, Vol. 23, Issue 6, 2012, pp. 2565-2586.

[9] A. Khamis, A. Hussein, A. Elmogy, "Multi-Robot Task Allocation: A Review of the State-of-the-Art," in Studies in Computational Intelligence, vol. 604, 2015, pp. 31–51.

[10] K. Karur, N. Sharma, C. Dharmatti, J. E. Siegel, "A survey of path planning algorithms for mobile robots," Vehicles, Vol. 3, Issue 3, 2021, pp. 448-468.

[11] S. El-Ansary, O. M. Shehata, E. S. I. Morgan, "Airport Management Controller: A Multi-Robot Task-Allocation Approach," Proc. of the 4th Int. Conf. on control, mechatronics and automation, 2017, pp. 26-30.

[12] M. De Ryck, M. Versteyhe, F. Debrouwere, "Automated guided vehicle systems, state-of-the-art control algorithms and techniques," J. of Manufacturing Systems, Vol. 54, 2020, pp. 152-173.

[13] A. Hussein and A. Khamis, "Market-based approach to multi-robot task allocation," Int. Conf. on Individual and Collective Behaviors in Robotics (ICBR), IEEE, 2013, pp. 69-74.

[14] S. Mariani, G. Cabri, F. Zambonelli, "Coordination of autonomous vehicles: Taxonomy and survey," ACM Computing Surveys (CSUR), Vol. 54, Issue 1, 2021, pp. 1-33.

[15] W. de Paula Ferreira, F. Armellini, L. A. De Santa-Eulalia, "Simulation in Industry 4.0: A State-of-the-Art Review," Computers & Industrial Eng., Vol. 149, 2020, pp. 106868.

[16] A. Daoud, F. Balbo, P. Gianessi, G. Picard, "ORNInA: A decentralized, auction-based multi-agent coordination in ODT systems," Ai Communications, Vol. 34, Issue 1, 2021, pp. 37-53.

[17] N.M. Kou, C. Peng, X. Yan, Z. Yang, "Multi-agent path planning with non-constant velocity motion," Proc. of the 18th Int. Conf. on Autonomous Agents and MultiAgent Systems, 2019, pp. 2069-2071.

[18] J. Grosset , A. Ndao, A.-J. Fougères, M. Djoko-Kouam, C. Couturier, J.-M. Bonnin, "A cooperative approach to avoiding obstacles and collisions between autonomous industrial vehicles in a simulation platform," Integrated Computer-Aided Engineering, Vol. 30, Issue 1, 2023, pp. 19–40.

[19] J. Grosset, A.-J. Fougères, M. Djoko-Kouam, J.-M. Bonnin, "Multi-agent Simulation of Autonomous Industrial Vehicle Fleets: Towards Dynamic Task Allocation in V2X Cooperation Mode," Integrated Computer-Aided Engineering, Vol. 31, Issue 3, 2024, pp. 249–266.

[20] V. Yerubandi, Y. M. Reddy, M. V. Kumar, "Navigation system for an autonomous robot using fuzzy logic," Int. j. of scientific and research pub., Vol. 5, Issue 2, 2015, pp. 5-8.

[21] A. Meylani, A. S. Handayani, R. S. Carlos, "Different Types of Fuzzy Logic in Obstacles Avoidance of Mobile Robot," I. Conf. on Electrical. Eng. and Comp. Sc., 2018, pp. 93-100.

[22] B. K. Patle, A. Pandey, D. R. K. Parhi, "A review: On path planning strategies for navigation of mobile robot," Defence Technology, Vol. 15, Issue 4, 2019, pp. 582-606.

[23] A. Nasrinahar and J. H. Chuah, "Intelligent motion planning of a mobile robot with dynamic obstacle avoidance," J. on Vehicle Routing Algorithms, Vol. 1, Issue 2, 2018, pp. 89-104.

[24] M. Alakhras, M. Oussalah, M. Hussein, "A survey of fuzzy logic in wireless localization," EURASIP J. on Wireless Com. and Networking, Vol. 1, 2020, pp. 1-45.

[25] M. F. R. Lee and A. Nugroho, "Intelligent Energy Management System for Mobile Robot," Sustainability, Vol. 14, Issue 16, 2022, 10056.

[26] E. Ostrosi, A.-J. Fougères, M. Ferney, "Fuzzy Agents for Product Configuration in Collaborative and Distributed Design Process," Applied Soft Computing, Vol. 8, Issue 12, 2012, pp. 2091–2105.

[27] L. A. Zadeh, "Fuzzy sets," Information and control, Vol. 8, Issue 3, 1965, pp. 338-353.

[28] H. M. Yudha, T. Dewi, N. Hasana, "Performance comparison of fuzzy logic and neural network design for mobile robot navigation," Int. Conf. on Electrical Eng. and Comp. Sc., 2019, pp. 79-84, 2019.

International Academy, Research, and Industry Association (IARIA)
412 Derby Way
Wilmington, DE 19810

ISBN 979-8-3313-0659-5

9 798331 306595

CURRAN ASSOCIATES INC.
proceedings.com

Fifteenth International Conference on Advanced Geographic Information Systems, Applications, and Services (GEOProcessing 2023)

Held at DigitalWorld 2023

Venice, Italy
24-28 April 2023

IARIA